Praise for *100 WAYS TO 1*
TODAY'S ECONOMY ...

We continue to receive feedback from our 2,400 CEO membership, saying how the ideas in Barry's book have helped them cut costs and save money.
—*W.E. Williams, Ph.D.*
President, The Executive Committee (TEC)

This exhaustive guide will greatly assist business managers in identifying and resolving multiple problems arising during turbulent times (and normal times, too.)
—*Irving Rudd, Adjunct Professor of*
Finance Emeritus, American University
Former President and C.E.O.
D.C. National Bank

... a logical outline any business can use in any economic climate to assess its strengths and weaknesses ... Provides the small businessman with the opportunity to review overall business operations at any time during the year, not just at the annual year end meeting.
—*Michael Tievy*
Gorelick, Tievy & Associates Inc.
Actuaries & Employee Benefit Consultants

100 WAYS TO PROSPER IN TODAY'S ECONOMY is a great compilation of practical, proven solutions to real business problems. There are no management philosophies or theoretical applications ... only common sense tested strategies to help a business particularly during tough times.
—*John J. Harkins*
Executive Vice President
Printing Industry of
Metropolitan Washington

... many good points that business people can use in these hard times.
—*Jay Dyer*
Commercial Banker

These steps helped us develop the work plan for our success in some very troubling times.
—*Michael C. Martin*
Dudley Martin Chevrolet, Inc.

Attention: Schools and Corporations
ACROPOLIS books are available at quantity discounts with bulk purchase for educational, business, or sales promotional use. For information, please write to: SPECIAL SALES DEPARTMENT, ACROPOLIS BOOKS LTD., 13950 Park Center Rd., Herdon, VA 22071.

Are there Acropolis books you want but cannot find in your local stores?
You can get any Acropolis book title in print. Simply send title and retail price. Be sure to add postage and handling: $2.25 for orders up to $15.00; $3.00 for orders from $15.01 to $30.00; $3.75 for orders from $30.01 to $100.00; $4.50 for orders over $100.00. District of Columbia residents add applicable sales tax. Enclose check or money order only, no cash please, to:

ACROPOLIS BOOKS LTD.
13950 Park Center Rd.
Herndon, VA 22071

Library of Congress Cataloging-in-Publication Data

Schimel, Barry R. 1941–
    100 ways to prosper in today's economy/ Barry R. Schimel.
        p. 230 cm.
    Includes index.
    ISBN 0-87491-984-3 : $18.95
    1. Small business--Finance. 2. Strategic planning.
3. Management. I. Title   II. Title: One hundred ways to
prosper in today's economy.
HG4027.7.S35   1991
658.02"2--dc20   91-29862
                                                            CIP

100
WAYS TO
PROSPER
IN TODAY'S ECONOMY

**BATTLE-TESTED BUSINESS STRATEGIES
THAT WORK NOW**

Barry R. Schimel, C.P.A.

Acropolis Books, Ltd.

CONTENTS

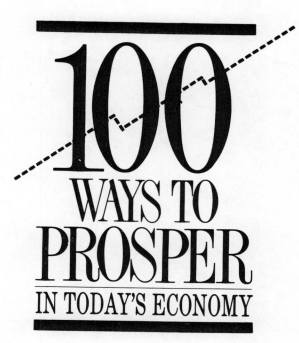

100
WAYS TO
PROSPER
IN TODAY'S ECONOMY

Introduction

100 Ways to Prosper in Today's Economy

Putting the "100 Ways" to Work for Your Business

Running a business is a risky proposition even in the best of times. When the economy sours and the market shrinks, the margin for error becomes that much narrower.

After more than 25 years as a Certified Public Accountant, I've been an eyewitness to the pain that businesses suffer during an economic downturn.

I've seen fortunes lost, dreams crushed, companies wiped out, and owners driven to consider suicide because of business reversals. But I've also helped many companies battle their way back from the brink. Good accountants don't just prepare tax returns and financial statements for businesses. Rather, they actively encourage their clients to share their business and financial problems—and work with them to find solutions to those problems.

Over the years we've worked with literally thousands of businesses large and small, from virtually every industry you can imagine. We've helped many of them become stronger organizations, but we've also learned a lot from those same companies.

Much of what we learned over the years is condensed into the following "100 Ways to Prosper in Today's Economy." This book is designed to

1

serve as a life preserver for businesses—particularly those struggling through their first full-blown recession.

The 1980s produced the longest period of sustained economic expansion in our nation's history. As a result, many people who started out in business during the past decade have never experienced an economic downturn. For these people, the economic climate of the 1990s is likely to be a particularly chilling experience.

There's no magic elixir that will restore the health of an ailing company, but there are strategies that businesses can use to survive until the turnaround takes hold. On the following pages you'll find 100 specific ideas that you can use to reduce overhead, attract new customers, secure financing, improve cash flow, and ultimately restore the profitability of your company.

Most of these "survival strategies" are just good business procedure—sound practices that will strengthen your organization during good times as well as bad. Indeed, if you put these principles to work at your firm, you're likely to have a stronger business after the recession than before.

I've tried to keep each chapter short, sweet and to the point. You won't find any general management theories or economic philosophizing in here—every one of these 100 chapters covers a battle-tested survival technique that has worked for other businesses.

For the most part, the examples that we've chosen to illustrate these points are taken directly from the case files of our firm. To be sure, we've altered some company descriptions to protect the confidentiality of our clients. But the problems we will discuss and solutions we'll share with you are real.

Not every one of the 100 survival ideas outlined in this book will be applicable to every business. Your job is to identify the strategies that pertain to your organization, and determine how to put the underlying concept to work at your company.

To make your work a little easier, there's a mini-action plan at the end of each chapter with space for you to jot down your ideas while they're still fresh. The form also calls for you to assign a priority (1 to 3) for each chapter, designate an individual in your organization to implement the recommendation, set a date for action, and project a potential dollar effect for your company.

At the end of the book you'll find a "Master Action Plan" that will help you coordinate the implementation of the approaches discussed in each of the chapters.

While this book can help you plot a course through the economic minefields, it can't work miracles. And it's no substitute for personal counseling by your CPA and other business advisers. The "100 Ways" are just the starting point.

Don't let that stop you from putting these survival strategies to use right now. Remember, as the owner or manager of a business, you have a responsibility to keep your organization alive and running even during the darkest hours.

Your duty isn't just to a "company." You have a responsibility to people who depend on you—your family, your employees, your shareholders, your suppliers and all the others who helped to build your organization.

I know you can do it. Now get to work!

Part I

Internal Cost Reduction

1. Identify Profit Centers, Keep the Winners, and Lose the Losers

Every business wants to increase sales during rough economic times, but some organizations have literally "sold" themselves into bankruptcy.

You know the old joke about the shopkeeper who sold everything in the store below his cost. "How can you stay in business?" someone asked. "Aren't you losing money on every sale?"

"Sure I am," he replied, "but I'll make it up in volume!"

Of course, you never "make it up in volume." The more goods or services you sell at a loss, the bigger your losses. A lot of businesses actually do operate this way unintentionally, because they don't bother to **identify key profit centers and eliminate marginal products or services.**

Unlike our overly generous shopkeeper, they may not sell everything at a loss. But even one or two poor pricing decisions can drain the profitability of an otherwise successful enterprise.

During good economic times when sales are booming these problems tend to go unnoticed. But when business turns sour and earnings go South, weeding out unprofitable goods or services can be one of the keys to survival.

The owner of a large chain of Italian restaurants put this strategy to work. His lasagna is terrific, the service is great, and it's a lot of fun to eat at one of his places. But when we conducted an analysis of his operations, we found that his menu prices were off the mark.

Some of the selections were priced at or below his cost of ingredients. Other dishes featured on the menu were so complicated and time-consuming to prepare that profits were wiped out by excess labor costs.

When the numbers were analyzed, the unprofitable dishes were exposed and their prices were increased. Our restaurateur then added some new mid-range selections to his menu—items like seafood pasta that could be priced reasonably yet still realize a good profit margin.

He ended up with a menu mix offering patrons a variety of meal choices and prices, while ensuring him a fair return no matter what they chose.

Isolating the major sources of profit and loss within your organization is an exercise that may well help you identify and correct other problems as well.

In another case, when a food wholesaler ran a detailed gross profit analysis of his operations, he discovered that some of the company's biggest ticket items yielded absolutely zero profits to the firm.

After combing through stacks of customer invoices and matching them with the cost of goods, we determined that the goods had been priced properly and that the wholesaler should have been realizing a substantial gross profit on their sale. Where did those profits go?

He concluded that the profit drain must be occurring as a result of pilferage. The wholesaler implemented new security measures and, sure enough, profits bounced back.

Point is: unless you undertake a gross profit analysis measuring the contribution from every major component of your product line, you may not even be aware that you have a problem.

STRATEGY NUMBER 1. Identify Profit Centers

HOW DOES THIS APPLY TO MY BUSINESS? _____

_____

_____

_____

_____

Priority   1   2   3   *(circle one)*   Action date _____

Potential dollar effect $ _____

Person assigned to this strategy _____

2. Be a "Hands-On" Manager

Over the years McDonald's has been able to sell hundreds of billions of hamburgers. One of the reasons for the chain's success: McDonald's is a franchise operation and the owner of each franchised restaurant is on the premises running the business.

That's not to say that every business requires the owner at the helm all the time. But in a bad economy when the company's survival is at stake, **the owner had better be on board—not just on call.**

Take the case of the absentee owner of a chain of gift shops. Although sales had fallen off company-wide in response to the slumping economy, most of her stores were still operating in the black. One location, however, was faring far worse than the others and the owner wanted to close it down before it dragged the entire company under.

She had been "managing" this retail business by long distance for several years, and decided to spend some time at the "problem" location before shutting it down.

It didn't take long for her to identify the cause of the store's distress. The place was filthy, inventory wasn't being reordered on a timely basis, staff morale was non-existent, and the unit manager—who was being paid more than $100,000 a year to run this store—wasn't even there most of the time! In fact, the owner learned that the store was routinely being closed an hour or two early every day!

She fired the store manager and took charge of the operation personally. Within a week sales bounced back by one-third, and within a month the store was operating in the black again.

Granted, this is a dramatic example. But every owner or top manager can find some way to become more involved in the business during tough times when leadership can make a real difference.

Become more of a motivational force for your organization! Start attending staff meetings that you ordinarily pass up. Write an article for your company's internal newsletter—or start an employee newsletter if you don't have one. Go on customer calls with your sales reps. Spend some time on the assembly line, or the loading dock, or the sales floor. Let your people know that you're willing to roll up your sleeves and pitch in when the pinch is on.

STRATEGY NUMBER 2: Be a Hands-On Manager
HOW DOES THIS APPLY TO MY BUSINESS? _____

_____

_____

_____

_____

Priority   1   2   3   *(circle one)*   Action date _____

Potential dollar effect $ _____

Person assigned to this strategy _____

3. Recapture Estimated Income Tax Overpayments

If you're like a lot of people in business, you make estimated corporate tax payments to IRS based on the taxes you paid in the previous year. But if you're having a really bad year, you may have no income tax liability at all. In such circumstances, it's a bad economic decision to keep paying estimated income taxes.

Of course, it's not always possible to predict your company's annual income and tax liability at the beginning of the year. By the time you discover you're in trouble, you may have already made several quarterly estimated tax payments—money your business may desperately need over the next few months.

For instance, a publishing house was blindsided by a series of misfortunes during one tax year. The company's federal income tax liability for the previous year had been nearly $240,000, and the publisher had so far made two quarterly estimated tax payments of $60,000 each so far in the current year.

All of a sudden the roof fell in. The company's primary printer went out of business and the publisher wound up paying considerably more for these services at a different shop. Then the economy turned sour and book sales fell off sharply. To make matters worse, a major retail chain abruptly canceled orders for a large number of the company's titles. Next, several top authors jumped ship and signed on with a different publishing house. Finally, when it looked like things couldn't get any worse, the courts ordered the firm to pay $100,000 in damages as a result of a libel suit!

It was a nightmare. The year was a total loss! No matter what happened over the next six months, there was no way the publisher was going to finish the year in the black.

The fact that the company wouldn't have any tax liability for the year was small consolation. The publisher had already laid out $120,000 in estimated tax payments—money that the firm now needed desperately to remain solvent.

Fortunately, **businesses don't have to wait until they file their annual tax return to recover overpayments in estimated income taxes.**

By filing a Form 4466 you can secure a quick refund of overpaid estimated taxes. There are a few strings, however. The overpayment must be at least 10 percent of the expected tax liability and at least $500. Moreover, you must also submit a Form 1120 to "perfect" the claim.

Corporations that still owe taxes from the previous year can avoid having to make those payments if they anticipate a loss in the current year. Firms facing such unhappy circumstances should file a form 1138 and claim a net operating loss carryback.

The form 1138 extends the time of payment of the previous year's tax liability because the expected net operating loss for the current year, when carried back, will either reduce or eliminate the previous year's tax liability.

Believe me, the paperwork is worth the trouble. When you're struggling to keep your business alive, there's no excuse for offering the government an interest free loan!

STRATEGY NUMBER 3: Recapture Estimated Income Tax Payments

HOW DOES THIS APPLY TO MY BUSINESS? _____

_____

_____

_____

_____

Priority   1   2   3   *(circle one)*   Action date _____

Potential dollar effect $ _____

Person assigned to this strategy _____

4. Recover Past Tax Payments by "Carrying Back" This Year's Loss

A lot of businesses that have experienced nothing but success and growth over the years simply don't know how to respond to a downturn. For many companies accustomed to nothing but black ink, a loss at the end of the year can come as a real shock.

With a little creative accounting, a loss at the end of the year can actually generate a healthy transfusion of cash for your business!

An important (though often overlooked) section of **the tax code allows corporations to "carryback" losses and effectively recalculate their tax liability for the previous three years.**

If your company paid taxes in any or all of the last three years, the government allows you to carry that loss back and retroactively reduce your tax liability for those profitable years.

You could actually recoup every penny of the taxes you paid over the past three years. For a financially-troubled business, this lifesaving maneuver could be money from heaven!

Suppose your company is struggling to keep afloat, but not actually running in the red. Since you don't have a loss to carry back, you're out of luck. Or are you?

Let's say your profitability has plunged to the break-even point after experiencing three successful years during which you paid an average of $20,000 in federal income taxes on income averaging $75,000 annually. With creative tax planning, you might be able to postpone sales until the next tax year, and at the same time accelerate expenses so that you're able to incur them this year.

Let's assume further that you're on the accrual basis of accounting for tax purposes, and that you are able to delay a transaction that will yield $200,000 in gross profit until the next tax year. Additionally, suppose that you accelerate $50,000 of operating expenses into the current tax year.

Through a little tax planning you would go from a break-even situation this year to one in which you're able to report a tax loss of $250,000. That loss could then be carried back to each of the three prior years, and your business would be able to recover the entire $60,000 in taxes that you paid to IRS during those years!

There is a catch, of sorts. Carrying back a tax loss can make a business appear financially weaker on paper. Be sure to explain what you're doing to your banker (see Chapter 35) to protect your credit standing.

STRATEGY NUMBER 4: Recover Past Tax Payments by "Carrying Back" this Year's Loss

HOW DOES THIS APPLY TO MY BUSINESS? _____

_____

_____

_____

_____

Priority   1   2   3   *(circle one)*   Action date _____

Potential dollar effect $ _____

Person assigned to this strategy _____

5. Cut Back Owners' Compensation

When business gets bad enough to warrant asking your employees to make some sacrifices, you as the owner had better be prepared to do some belt-tightening of your own. Certainly if conditions warrant such drastic actions as reducing wage rates or eliminating employee bonuses, **the first person to take a pay cut should be the boss.**

If the staff realizes that the big boss is willing to take a pay cut for the good of the firm, then they'll be more willing to accept the sacrifices necessary to keep the company afloat. Indeed, it is axiomatic that when a business is healthy, the individual who feeds off it, the owner, will also be healthy. But when the economy is sick and the business is at death's door, it's time for fasting, not feasting.

The owner who tries to squeeze too much out of his business for his own personal use will likely wind up killing the golden goose.

As a rule of thumb, if economic conditions mandate drastic action, the owners of the business should trim back their compensation to a level that approximates their necessary living expenses. You will have to judge what's "necessary" for you and your family, but during hard times all of us can pull in our belt a little and live a bit leaner than in the past.

A couple who owned several retail stores, paid a terrible price to learn this lesson. The business had developed into a highly successful operation, and the owners had become accustomed to a lavish and luxurious lifestyle. Every year each of them bought a new luxury car, they took extensive vacations at jet-set resorts, had several houses, and so on.

In good times the business could sustain this lifestyle, but when the economy turned sour it was clearly time for the owners to put an end to their conspicuous consumption. Despite the business downturn, however, our clients continued to draw large salaries. Almost inevitably the business went down the tubes, and the owners had to sell their home and start all over again.

Worse yet, the financial pressures associated with the collapse of the business took a heavy toll on the owners personally. In the end, the business wasn't the only thing destroyed—so was their marriage.

STRATEGY NUMBER 5: Cut Back Owners' Compensation
HOW DOES THIS APPLY TO MY BUSINESS? _____

_____

_____

_____

_____

Priority   1   2   3   *(circle one)*   Action date _____
Potential dollar effect $ _____
Person assigned to this strategy _____

6. Start Signing All Checks Personally

Do you really know who's spending your money in your company? Or what they're buying? Or whether they're getting their money's worth? There's only one way of finding the answers to these questions. In tough times, it should be standard operating procedure for the owner or CEO of the business to **personally sign every check for every expenditure.**

Many of you do this already. If you aren't signing the checks, try it and you'll be astonished at what you'll find out. Where did those extra 30 boxes of coffee filters come from? Who ordered eighteen shipments of ball point pens? Why is there a car rental bill from an agency in the Bahamas, when all your clients are in Milwaukee?

It's likely that you'll find a significant amount of waste —the remnants of extravagant practices that date back to better times, but can't be justified under present conditions.

Just in time, the owner of a financially-troubled travel agency took control of his company's checkbook, and discovered a variety of disturbing activities. There were prompt payment discounts that could have been taken by his business, but were not because the bills were paid late. Other bills, meanwhile, were being paid before they were due. The company was missing out on quantity discounts because orders were not being consolidated. Employees were working overtime, at premium pay, during periods when there should have been little for them to do.

Simply by getting a handle on the obvious waste, the owner was able to maneuver the agency back into the black.

In another case, a company regularly ordered bottled water for its employees. It was a little office luxury that had begun several years earlier when business was booming. As soon as the owner started signing the company checks, he realized that this "little" luxury was soaking up $250 a month—money that could certainly be put to better use by the cash-strapped company. The owner promptly canceled the deliveries, installed water purifiers on the faucets of the office, and reduced operating costs by almost $3,000 a year.

The owner of a firm with almost 60 employees had a real brainstorm the first time she wrote out the monthly check to pay the company's health insurance policy. The business was paying premiums for every one of them. Certainly some of these employees were covered under their spouse's health insurance policy?

The owner checked it out and, sure enough, the company was paying premiums to duplicate coverage for over a dozen people. Now employees who receive health insurance benefits at this firm must first sign a statement certifying that they are not already covered by their spouse's policy.

The bottom line is that the company was able to reduce its insurance costs by more than $35,000 a year.

STRATEGY NUMBER 6: Start Signing All Checks Personally
HOW DOES THIS APPLY TO MY BUSINESS? ⎯⎯⎯⎯⎯⎯⎯⎯⎯

⎯⎯⎯⎯⎯⎯⎯⎯⎯⎯⎯⎯⎯⎯⎯⎯⎯⎯⎯⎯⎯⎯⎯⎯⎯⎯⎯⎯⎯⎯⎯⎯

⎯⎯⎯⎯⎯⎯⎯⎯⎯⎯⎯⎯⎯⎯⎯⎯⎯⎯⎯⎯⎯⎯⎯⎯⎯⎯⎯⎯⎯⎯⎯⎯

⎯⎯⎯⎯⎯⎯⎯⎯⎯⎯⎯⎯⎯⎯⎯⎯⎯⎯⎯⎯⎯⎯⎯⎯⎯⎯⎯⎯⎯⎯⎯⎯

⎯⎯⎯⎯⎯⎯⎯⎯⎯⎯⎯⎯⎯⎯⎯⎯⎯⎯⎯⎯⎯⎯⎯⎯⎯⎯⎯⎯⎯⎯⎯⎯

Priority   1   2   3   *(circle one)*   Action date ⎯⎯⎯⎯⎯⎯
Potential dollar effect $ ⎯⎯⎯⎯⎯⎯⎯⎯⎯⎯⎯⎯⎯⎯⎯⎯⎯⎯⎯⎯⎯⎯
Person assigned to this strategy ⎯⎯⎯⎯⎯⎯⎯⎯⎯⎯⎯⎯⎯⎯⎯⎯⎯

7. Limit Expense Authorization to Upper Management

One way to combat the effects of a business recession is to work harder by producing and selling more goods and services. That's fine, and it's certainly important to maximize every business opportunity during a slump. But when a company fills more orders and generates more sales volume, very few of those gross dollars come down to the bottom line where you need them.

Last year, for example, the average supermarket had to sell $100 worth of groceries to make 86 cents in net income! Profitability figures vary from industry to industry, of course, but most businesses are lucky to bring 5 cents on the dollar down to the bottom line.

In contrast, when you save money by reducing operating expenses, 100 percent of those dollars go directly down to the net profit line.

Look at it this way. Your best salesman might knock himself out for months to bring in an additional $100,000 in sales. At a 5 percent net profit, those extra sales will bring $5,000 to the bottom line. But by managing operating costs more effectively, many businesses can easily realize a similar gain in profitability.

It's not unusual for a company to spend, say, $50,000 a year on supplies. But it's much easier to reduce these expenses 10 percent through more effective management, than it is to generate $100,000 in new sales through elbow grease and shoe leather.

One of the surest ways to reduce operating costs is for the boss to personally control expenses. If upper management approves expenses, then the manager or owner can take responsibility for what's happening in his department. How many times have you come across questionable expenditures after the fact? By then it's too late.

Take a close look at your company's purchasing procedures. Are you working from a purchase order system? Can just anybody place orders? Or must they be approved in a systematic manner before supplies are requisitioned?

A commercial glass installer learned this lesson the hard way. The company had 15 different locations, and each office was individually responsible for ordering pens, pencils, paper and other office supplies. Every month they were placing orders for six to seven thousand different supply items, all various grades and prices, and the waste was enormous. The attitude at the branch office was, "If I need something, I'll just pick it out of the catalog, regardless of price, or quality or quantity."

Top management finally sat down with the firm's chief supplier and together they hammered out a standard supply order form that offered one choice for each category. Suddenly, expenditures for cases of $2.49 felt tip pens stopped. When branch offices ordered pens, they received 29-cent ball points.

STRATEGY NUMBER 7: Limit Expense Authorization to Upper Management

HOW DOES THIS APPLY TO MY BUSINESS? _____

_____

_____

_____

_____

Priority   1   2   3   *(circle one)*   Action date _____

Potential dollar effect $ _____

Person assigned to this strategy _____

8. Monitor Departmental Budgets

Many businesses make the mistake of establishing an overall company budget, but then fail to break that budget down by department. As a result, some divisions of the organization are chronically running over budget, while others are constantly being squeezed. Once you've worked out an operating budget for your organization as a whole, **set individual budgets for each department or branch, and hold department heads accountable for those budgets.**

Let your divisional managers know that the rewards they can expect will depend on how successfully they use the resources budgeted to them. If the manager marshals those resources effectively and the department is successful, that individual deserves to share in the fruits of success through bonuses or other forms of compensation.

That's only good business sense, but you would be surprised at how many organizations don't operate this way. Failing to establish budget goals on a department by department basis can create chaos within a company. I know of businesses that have been literally crippled because they neglected to do this.

Take the case of the publishing company that budgeted $100,000 for legal expenses during the year. The company's magazine division encountered some legal claims which could have been resolved quickly for well under $5,000. Instead of settling, however, the department decided to fight the claim and retained a law firm. Unfortunately for the publisher, the legal expenses exceeded estimates and by the time the dispute was finally resolved, the company's entire legal budget had been exhausted.

Later that same year the publisher's textbook division encountered a legal pothole of its own. At that point, however, the cupboard was bare, the publisher's legal budget was gone. Through no fault of their own, the people in the textbook division were left to choose between several equally unappealing options.

The root cause of these problems was the fact that the publisher did not set departmental budgets and did not hold its divisional managers accountable for those budgets. The people in the magazine division regarded the corporate legal services budget as Other Peoples' Money! Rather than spending $5,000 of the division's "own money" to settle a claim, they chose to spend $100,000 in "OPM" to fight it!

The failure to hold business managers responsible for their own budgets can create other problems within an organization.

Suppose, for example, we take an automobile dealership and organize it into a new car department, a used car department, and a service department. Let's say the dealer's overall advertising budget for the year is $500,000. If at the start of the year the new car department contracts for ad placements costing $500,000, there's nothing left in the kitty for the used car manager or the service manager to promote their departments.

The owner would then have to decide whether to come up with additional money for advertising, or to allow the used car sales and service departments to suffer for lack of promotional funds.

In this case, besides creating serious problems for the company, the absence of departmental budgets leads to a grossly unfair situation for middle managers whose income is linked to the performance of their departments.

The correct way to handle this situation would be for the dealership to earmark, say, $300,000 for new car advertising, and $100,000 each for used cars and service. But then what's to stop the new car manager from spending most or all of the department's ad budget during the first quarter, leaving little left for the rest of the year? Nothing! But perhaps that would be a wise decision given the market conditions at the time. In any event, you've hired that manager to make those decisions. If you lack confidence in a particular manager's judgment, replace that person with someone you do trust. Most of all, make your department chiefs aware that they will be held accountable for using the resources budgeted to them to perform successfully.

STRATEGY NUMBER 8: Monitor Departmental Budgets
HOW DOES THIS APPLY TO MY BUSINESS? _____
_____
_____
_____
_____

Priority   1   2   3   *(circle one)*   Action date _____
Potential dollar effect $ _____
Person assigned to this strategy _____

9. Monitor Personal Use of Company Cars

Businesses that provide company cars or other vehicles for use by employees often incur an alarming amount of unnecessary expense. It's not unusual to find that 20 to 30 percent of the cost of providing these vehicles reflects non-business use or outright waste.

Even if you lease the vehicle, when you factor in such operating expenses as gasoline, maintenance, repairs and insurance, it's going to cost your company at least $5,000 to $10,000 per year to keep each one on the road. If even 10 percent of these costs are unnecessary, a significant amount of company profit is escaping down the rathole. In the best of times, a waste factor of $500 to $1,000 a year per vehicle should be considered a misdemeanor. In a bad year, to allow such losses to continue unchecked is a capital offense.

At a minimum, **employees should be expected to maintain a daily travel log** listing all mileage driven, destinations, and the reason for each trip.

Such procedures will not only help you reduce waste, but may also enable you to uncover more serious problems within your organization. One business that tightened vehicle-use record keeping discovered that one of its drivers was systematically siphoning gasoline from the company truck he drove home every night. We estimate that during the past two years the business lost at least $30 a week from this gas thief. Certainly, that $3,000 could have been put to better use.

A policy of limiting company vehicles to business use could do more than reduce your operating costs, however. It could also protect your business from nightmare liability. Suppose an employee driving home in a company car stopped off for a few drinks and then caused an accident. Imagine the exposure your company would face.

It may not be practical to flatly prohibit all personal use of business vehicles. But at a minimum, employees who put company vehicles to personal use should be asked to absorb a proportion of the costs.

If you permit employees to drive company cars home, personal use should be monitored and the driver should be charged for mileage not attributable to business.

Even if you impose only a token charge for non-business mileage, at least you're serving notice to your employees that you're concerned about excessive or unnecessary use of company cars.

In some ways, technological advancement is underscoring the need to keep tight control over automobile costs. Last year a business associate of mine installed cellular telephones in each company car used by his outside sales force. No doubt the car phones added to the productivity of the sales reps. But they also created new opportunities for waste and abuse of company funds.

We analyzed the client's telephone use and were able to trace at least one-third of the company's total charges to the cellular phones. We found that the car phones were being used to order pizzas, call 900 numbers, and make non-business long-distance calls. The owner was astonished.

To put an end to this waste, the company adopted a new system under which all calls made on these car phones had to be logged in. Actually, such logs are required by IRS to verify the deductibility of these calls. Under the procedures, employees are still allowed to make personal calls on company car phones, but the cost of those calls is deducted from their paychecks.

STRATEGY NUMBER 9: Monitor Personal Use of Company Cars

HOW DOES THIS APPLY TO MY BUSINESS? _____

_____

_____

_____

_____

Priority   1   2   3   *(circle one)*   Action date _____

Potential dollar effect $ _____

Person assigned to this strategy _____

10. Link Bonuses to Performance

Make no mistake, an employee bonus—whether it's cash, or a gift, or time off, or something else of value—can be a powerful tool to motivate a workforce. But an employee bonus can also be a colossal waste of money. Worse yet, the wrong kind of bonus can backfire on a business and become a minefield of employee resentment and hostility toward management.

There are two types of employee bonuses: those that encourage your people to become more productive or maintain high standards of performance, and those that do not. The rule of thumb is simple in this case: **either link employee bonuses to performance, or eliminate them altogether.**

Fortunately, it's easy to distinguish between the two types of employee bonuses. Remember, you're trying to encourage certain types of behavior by rewarding it. For example, consider offering a bonus to:

- salesmen who exceed their quotas for the year;
- service department personnel who complete a higher than average number of procedures;
- accounts receivable staffers who achieve high levels of collections;
- production line workers who suggest product design improvements;
- or any employees who consistently report to work on time, or use less than their allotment of sick leave, or suggest ways to reduce expenses.

In each of these examples, extending bonuses creates two winners: the employee who receives the compensation and the employer who benefits from the worker's positive performance.

On the other hand, what does an employer accomplish by offering Christmas bonuses, or year end bonuses, or other forms of extra compensation not dependent on the employee's performance? Free-floating bonuses that aren't attached to positive performance can create serious problems for struggling businesses.

What happens, for example, when business takes a nosedive and management can no longer afford to offer holiday bonuses? Employees who received those goodies in the past, continue to expect them. And the bigger these bonuses are, the more potentially dangerous they become. I've seen corporations face outright mutiny because they attempted to discontinue their practice of offering hefty end-of-the-year bonuses.

While the best policy is not to offer non-performance linked bonuses in the first place, how do you dismount from the tiger once the ride has begun? My advice is to do it very gingerly.

You can't take a benefit away from a veteran employee. If you gave them each a turkey last year, you'd better give them a turkey this year, or else you'll be the turkey. But if you've been routinely passing out substantial cash bonuses unrelated to performance, put an end to the practice. Explain to your employees that from now on, the amount that they had been receiving at year end will go into their paychecks in the form of a salary increase spread over 52 weeks.

That way existing employees don't feel they're losing anything, and you're not obligated to offer future bonuses to new employees.

STRATEGY NUMBER 10: Link Bonuses to Performance

HOW DOES THIS APPLY TO MY BUSINESS? _____

_____

_____

_____

_____

Priority   1   2   3   *(circle one)*   Action date _____

Potential dollar effect $ _____

Person assigned to this strategy _____

11. Scale Back Retirement Plan Contributions

A retirement plan is one of the most important benefits you can offer to valued people in your organization. These plans not only enable you to reward long-time employees, but also encourage newcomers to sink roots and build a career with your company.

But make no mistake: business-as-usual company contributions retirement plans can be a costly luxury in a stormy economy. Given the option of cutting pension plan contributions or cutting employees, your choice should be clear. If you offer a defined benefit pension plan, the administrators of these plans can often "massage" the actuarial assumptions and allow you to temporarily reduce or skip your contributions to the plan.

Suppose, for example, that when the plan was established it was based on the actuarial assumption that contributions paid into the plan would yield an average annual return of 6 percent. If it turned out that the actual return on these contributions has been 12 percent, the company may be perfectly justified in temporarily reducing payments or skipping some contributions altogether.

Regardless of the actuarial justifications, however, **cutting back on pension plan contributions may be preferable to other alternatives available to a struggling company.**

We represent an advertising agency that was very successful for a number of years. During the good times, the principals shared the wealth by making very generous annual contributions to the company's employee profit sharing plan.

When the recession hit and billings dried up, the agency continued to make substantial retirement plan contributions. Management believed that employees had come to expect these benefits, and that even a temporary break from the routine would prompt a mutiny among the troops.

Given the seriousness of the agency's financial problems, we convinced the firm to reduce its retirement plan contributions by approximately 50 percent. As it turned out, there was no staff mutiny. The employees realized that the agency was struggling through a difficult period, and they took the attitude that 50 percent was still a lot better than zero, and it was far better than an outright salary reduction.

To be sure, there was a little grumbling after the reduced pension contribution was announced, but even the complainers recognized that many companies don't offer any retirement benefits.

Indeed, a number of businesses have abandoned retirement programs in response to the shaky economy. In addition to eliminating annual contributions, these employers have also saved the often significant legal, accounting and other administrative costs associated with employee pension plans.

When the assets of a retirement plan are liquidated and the funds are dispersed to the participants, employees may then "roll over" that lump sum payment into an Individual Retirement Account. This way, no tax is imposed on the funds until they're withdrawn from the IRA upon retirement.

STRATEGY NUMBER 11: Scale Back Retirement Plan Contributions

HOW DOES THIS APPLY TO MY BUSINESS? _____

_____

_____

_____

_____

Priority   1   2   3   *(circle one)*   Action date _____

Potential dollar effect $ _____

Person assigned to this strategy _____

12. Reward Employees With Non-Cash Compensation

When the economy is strong and business is really humming, it's appropriate to reward productive workers with salary increases or cash bonuses.

In bad times, however, cash may not be available to spread around. Fortunately, money isn't the only motivational tool at your disposal. In fact, studies have found that non-monetary compensation is an even more important factor for many people.

The satisfaction that comes from being recognized as an important and valued associate is an extremely powerful motivator for your employees. A new job title that reflects an individual's increased contributions to the organization, a private office, business cards, a person's name on the door, the opportunity to attend professional meetings—these are all motivators that cost a company little if anything out of pocket. Yet they can help maintain or even enhance staff morale during troubled times.

In addition, there are also some tangible forms of compensation that you can offer your employees during times when cash is short.

One strategy that we urge our clients to consider when money is tight is to offer employees "phantom stock" in lieu of cash bonuses. Unlike regular common stock, phantom stock does not convey any equity in the business. But it does enable the employee to share in any future appreciation in the value of the business.

For example, let's take the case of a business worth $500,000. The owner issues one share of "phantom stock" equal to 1 percent of the future appreciation of the business to each of 10 employees. If the value of the business eventually increases to $800,000, each share of "phantom stock" will then be worth $3,000 (1 percent of the $300,000 appreciation).

It's a good deal for employees because they will have the opportunity to participate in the increased value of the company, and a motivation to enhance the profitability of the business. A phantom stock program is a good deal for the owner, as well, because the business can conserve cash by deferring compensation to a future date without giving away any ownership in the company.

Another technique we recommend is to form an Employee Stock Ownership Plan (ESOP) enabling your workers to earn a retirement nest egg, which will grow as the business prospers. This is another approach that offers employees a real incentive to help the company succeed.

But an ESOP can also be a great deal for the owner of a business. The owner can sell some of his stock in the company to the ESOP, reinvest the proceeds in publicly-held securities, and not pay any tax on the gain until the stock is sold.

It's a win-win situation!

STRATEGY NUMBER 12: Reward Employees With Non-Cash Compensation

HOW DOES THIS APPLY TO MY BUSINESS? _____

_____

_____

_____

_____

Priority   1   2   3   *(circle one)*   Action date _____

Potential dollar effect $ _____

Person assigned to this strategy _____

13. Eliminate Unnecessary Utility Costs

Many businesses have gone down the tubes because management failed to curb wasteful energy use. Even if you rent your building space, chances are you have a triple net lease that will result in higher rent payments if utility costs rise.

For years, a furniture retailer deliberately left all the lights burning in the showroom. It cost the store at least $500 a month to do this, but the owner justified the expense as a form of "advertising." Customers who drove past the store when the lights were blazing late at night would surely remember the place, he reasoned.

Ultimately, he was convinced that there are more cost-effective methods of building customer recognition for his business. He bought a beautiful neon sign that offered ten times the exposure of his lit-up showroom at one-tenth the cost. As it turned out the store paid for the sign out of electricity savings during the first three years.

The management company of a medical office was wasting the owner's money because some of the tenants kept evening hours and left the air conditioning running all night.

The extent of the problem didn't become clear, however, until several of the internists and gynecologists in the building began losing patients. It seemed the building was so chilly in the morning that disrobed patients were getting goosebumps!

This building operator consulted a specialist in the air conditioning and heating area, and invested more than $25,000 in a computer system to regulate temperatures in offices year round. That was six years ago, and although it seemed like a lot of money at the time, the energy savings paid for the system in less than three years. Since then, it's been pure gravy.

You probably don't need a $25,000 computer to shave your utility bills. **There are automatic setback thermostats that will turn off your heat or air conditioning in the evening** after everyone has left the building, then turn it on again in the morning before anyone arrives.

A word of caution, though: utility experts warn that it is possible for energy-conscious building operators to outsmart themselves. The cost of reheating some facilities is so high that it more than offsets any savings from turning the utilities off at night. In these cases, the most efficient approach is to set the thermostat at one temperature and leave it there 24 hours a day.

STRATEGY NUMBER 13: Eliminate Unnecessary Utility Costs

HOW DOES THIS APPLY TO MY BUSINESS? _____

_____

_____

_____

_____

Priority   1   2   3   *(circle one)*   Action date _____

Potential dollar effect $ _____

Person assigned to this strategy _____

14. Sublet Unused Office Space

Typically, managers respond to tough times by trying to increase sales. But that's only one way to survive a bad economy. **Reducing a company's ongoing operating expenses is often the shortest route back to profitability.**

Even major "uncontrollable" expenses such as rent can be harnessed. Indeed, when sales are down a company may require less production, fewer employees, less inventory . . . and therefore less space. Why not identify that excess space—an empty room in an office, an unused section of a warehouse, an idle assembly line in a factory—and lease it to someone who can use it!

You'd be surprised at the kind of space that others will pay for. One business even managed to turn some unused parking spaces on a back lot into extra profits. A nearby bank with a limited parking area was more than willing to rent the vacant spaces to keep employee cars off its lot.

Sometimes you can rent out business space or facilities for short-term idle periods. A new car dealer didn't have enough weekend business to keep his service department open on Saturdays and Sundays. He decided to rent out his service bays on those days—along with a mechanic—on a flat rate basis to businesses with their own fleets of vehicles.

For the fleet owners, it was an opportunity to have their vehicles serviced during a non-workday . . . and at a flat bargain rate. For the dealer, it was a chance to off-set some of his occupancy costs . . . and to develop a business relationship with area fleet operators who, sooner or later, will be in the market for new vehicles.

Remember, too, that the market value of your idle space may increase significantly if you're able to throw in a few additional services that you're paying for anyway.

A law firm with an idle office may be able to rent it out for, say, $500 a month. But if the firm throws in access to a law library, a receptionist, a photocopy machine, a fax machine and a conference room—things that the firm is paying for anyway —the market value of that office may jump to $1,000 or $1,500 per month.

If you can't find a renter for your unused space, perhaps you can come up with a productive use for it yourself. A retail luggage chain operates a large distribution center to service their stores. But when sales softened and inventory requirements declined, the owner found herself with excess warehouse space.

Her response was to partition off part of the distribution center, and open it to the public on weekends as a clearance outlet for old inventory from the stores. The public loved the "bargain prices," and the chain was able to boost sales without incurring additional overhead costs.

STRATEGY NUMBER 14: Sublet Unused Office Space

HOW DOES THIS APPLY TO MY BUSINESS? _____

_____

_____

_____

_____

Priority   1   2   3   *(circle one)*   Action date _____

Potential dollar effect $ _____

Person assigned to this strategy _____

15. Dispose of Slow Moving and Obsolete Inventory

In every business there are hits and misses—hot selling goods or services and real dogs that nobody seems to want. Often, the difference between a business's success or failure is the ability to distinguish between the two, and the courage to **cut losses quickly by disposing of the doggies.**

Because time is money, the key word is "quickly." As a rule of thumb, we figure that the expense of maintaining goods in inventory averages about 2 percent of the cost of those goods each month. If you carry an item in stock on the shelves or in a warehouse for a year, you're down 24 percent. There aren't many businesses that can overcome this kind of a cost handicap even in the best of times. When business is bad, a slow moving inventory can be a killer.

For many business people, however, disposing of obsolete inventory is difficult because it means they have to admit making a mistake. Some have gone to the grave without making that admission.

One businesswoman who inherited a small gift shop in a resort area was surprised when she paid a visit to the store. The shelves were crammed with a lot of dingy looking merchandise that seemed to be priced far too low.

Upon closer inspection she discovered why. Based on the price tags, some of the goods had to have been sitting on those shelves for at least 15 years! But even at prices from the 1970s, this shopworn merchandise was no bargain. Indeed, much of the inventory was virtually unsalable.

She donated most of the merchandise to charity, sold the rest at a distress sale, and restocked the store with fresh inventory. Today the shop is a viable business again, and the owner has an iron-clad policy of getting rid of dogs. If an item doesn't sell in six months, she cuts the price 40 percent and moves it out.

In some industries, it's possible to work out arrangements with suppliers to limit your vulnerability to slow-selling inventories. An auto parts retailer established a relationship with a wholesaler that allowed the store to return any unsold merchandise for full credit within a year.

Unfortunately, however, the company's warehouse manager failed to keep records necessary to establish the purchase date of merchandise in stock. In reviewing the business's inventory the owner discovered thousands of dollars of old, obsolete parts sitting alongside new merchandise.

Had these old goods been identified in time, they could have been returned to the supplier in exchange for fresh merchandise. Instead, the retailer wound up disposing of them for a few cents on the dollar.

STRATEGY NUMBER 15: Dispose of Slow Moving and Obsolete Inventory

HOW DOES THIS APPLY TO MY BUSINESS? _____

_____

_____

_____

_____

Priority   1   2   3   *(circle one)*   Action date _____

Potential dollar effect $ _____

Person assigned to this strategy _____

16. Reward Your Employees for Bright Ideas

You can read this book cover-to-cover, but the best source of advice on how to survive a bad economy may be right under your nose. It's your own workforce.

Your employees know where the bottlenecks are in your organization, and they have some very interesting ideas for trimming costs, building sales and improving products or services.

But employees aren't always willing or able to articulate those ideas. Face facts: if the atmosphere in your organization discourages people from reporting or acknowledging problems, it's also going to discourage them from suggesting solutions. Your job is to **create a climate where your employees are motivated to make suggestions that can help the business.**

Here is a really effective way to secure input from employees. In effect, it's a way to systematize the old employee "suggestion box" concept. Periodically, ask everyone on your staff to fill out a form which asks for their input from three different perspectives. All employees are given a worksheet requesting that they jot down:

- ideas to improve the firm;
- ideas to improve their department; and
- ideas to improve their own performance.

It's essential that this be done in writing, and it's important to insist that they come up with five suggestions in each category. We've found that the first one or two answers are the easy, obvious ideas—the really creative suggestions tend to surface after the superficial ones are out of the way.

Once you've undertaken this exercise, take the time to explain which suggestions will be used, and why others will be rejected. It's important to let your people know that you value their advice and appreciate their ideas— even the ones you can't accept.

It's also a good idea to reward employees for brainstorming on behalf of the company. If a staff suggestion brings in new business or reduces operating costs, a cash bonus is certainly in order. But remember that money isn't the only motivator. The possibilities include recognition in the company house organ or at the next staff meeting, a day off, an "employee of the month" award, a plaque acknowledging the individual's contributions— the list goes on and on.

(STAFF MEMBER MAKING SUGGESTIONS)

Please list five ideas for each of the following:

SUGGESTIONS FOR IMPROVING THE FIRM

1 _____

2 _____

3 _____

4 _____

5 _____

SUGGESTIONS FOR IMPROVING YOUR DEPARTMENT

1 _____

2 _____

3 _____

4 _____

5 _____

SUGGESTIONS FOR IMPROVING YOUR ROLE WITHIN THE FIRM

1 _____

2 _____

3 _____

4 _____

5 _____

STRATEGY NUMBER 16: Reward Your Employees for Bright Ideas

HOW DOES THIS APPLY TO MY BUSINESS? _____

_____

_____

_____

_____

Priority   1   2   3   *(circle one)*   Action date _____

Potential dollar effect $ _____

Person assigned to this strategy _____

17. Guard Against Losses from Employee Theft

When times are tough for your business, your employees may also be experiencing economic difficulties of their own. If the temptations become too great, and the opportunities are there, employee theft could add to your business woes.

During bad times it is particularly important to **establish adequate controls to discourage employee theft.** You need systems and procedures that make it difficult if not impossible for any one worker to steal company funds or property without being in collusion with another employee. Whenever it takes the involvement of two or more people to steal from an employer, the odds of being victimized by employee theft get much longer.

A major building contractor had a bookkeeper who was robbing the company blind, and getting away with it because of a lack of proper controls. Although the owner of the company made it a rule to personally approve and sign all checks, the bookkeeper was able to find an easy way around that.

When she presented the owner with an invoice and asked for his signature on the check, she had carbon paper and a blank check underneath. She would then destroy the original check, trace over the carbon signature on the second check with a felt tip pen, and make it payable to herself for the exact amount of the original.

When we became the accountants for this organization, one of the first things we did was to separate duties so that an employee other than the bookkeeper was responsible for reconciling the company's check records with each monthly bank statement.

Within a month we discovered the scheme, but by then the larcenous bookkeeper had quit her job and mysteriously dropped from sight. Fortunately, our client was covered by a blanket fidelity bond and therefore recovered the losses from the insurance carrier. But even so, it was a painful lesson that this business owner had to learn the hard way.

STRATEGY NUMBER 17: Guard Against Losses from Employee Theft

HOW DOES THIS APPLY TO MY BUSINESS? _____

_____

_____

_____

_____

Priority   1   2   3   *(circle one)*   Action date _____

Potential dollar effect $ _____

Person assigned to this strategy _____

18. Lock the Supply Closet

Figure out how much your business spends on supplies in a typical year, multiply that total by 40 percent, and I'll bet you would have a pretty good estimate of the amount you could save by placing tighter controls over these materials.

I'm not suggesting that employees are likely to be raiding the company's supplies for their own personal use—although that certainly has happened at some firms. I am, however, suggesting that **an unregulated supply closet is likely to be an engine of waste within any organization.**

Look around your office or shop and notice how supplies are being used. In our office, I'm one of the worst offenders. I looked around my house one day and found 19 company pens that I had carried home over the past few weeks without even realizing it!

The first step toward correcting this problem is to padlock your supply cabinets and assign one person in the organization responsibility for these items. To obtain supplies, employees should be asked to fill out a short requisition form. This not only gives you a way to get a handle on where these items are going, but it also serves as a reminder to employees that the availability of company supplies is not unlimited.

Be forewarned, though. If you've been allowing unrestricted access to supplies, when you finally do impose controls on these items count on some grumbling from your staff.

A law firm was budgeting an excessive amount for office supplies. There were fewer than 50 employees at this particular office, yet the firm was spending almost $30,000 a year on stationery, pens, pencils and other routine supplies. It was easy to see why costs were so high. The supply room was unsecured, people were allowed to walk in and grab whatever they wanted, and the place was a complete mess.

When the partners imposed controls over the office supply closet, there were plenty of complaints. Some employees accused the firm of penny-pinching; others viewed the new procedures as an indication that they were not trusted.

But the partners were able to nip that resentment in the bud by pointing out that the purpose of the new system was not simply to bring expenses in line. They explained that these procedures would also streamline the ordering process and keep the supply room neat.

The staff complaints stopped, and so did much of the waste. Thanks to the new procedures, the lawyers were able to slice their supply costs in half and realize a tidy $15,000 a year savings.

STRATEGY NUMBER 18: Lock the Supply Cabinets

HOW DOES THIS APPLY TO MY BUSINESS? _____

_____

_____

_____

_____

Priority   1   2   3   *(circle one)*   Action date _____

Potential dollar effect $ _____

Person assigned to this strategy _____

19. Use a Fax Machine to Speed Collections and Trim Expenses

In a weak economy, the difference between survival and extinction is often the ability of the company to collect from customers quickly. Fortunately, you have technology on your side.

For my money, one of the most cost effective business machines that any organization can own today is a facsimile transmitter/receiver. A "fax" machine isn't just a glorified telephone—it's a messenger service, a post office, and a newsletter distribution service all in one. One company in our building saves wasted staff time at lunch hour by faxing carry-out orders to the local Chinese restaurant!

Chow mein isn't all a fax machine can get you, however. Take it from an accountant who has had to make changes on tax forms at zero hour—April 15th. Our firm would go crazy if we had to chase people down by phone and then dictate what we needed over the line. Federal Express doesn't cut it either; it takes too long, and it costs too much.

Instead, for only pennies a page, we get all the information we need zapped to us instantaneously by fax. **Faxing is cheaper, faster, and more effective than any other form of communication,** and in a bad economy this can be a lifesaver.

A local law firm saved a bundle when they stopped mailing their monthly client billing statements and started faxing them instead. This particular firm sends out roughly 1,200 statements a month. If you figure the cost of stamps at 29 cents, plus another nickel or so to cover stationary, the statements were costing at least 34 cents apiece.

That doesn't sound like that much, until you multiply it by the number of statements this law firm sent: 14,400 each year. That adds up to a tidy $4,464 in mailing expenses.

Even after the telephone line charges, paper costs and depreciation on the machine, faxing saved the firm at least $3,000 a year. The real advantage though, is that you get your bill to your client the day it is issued. The faster you get your bills out, the faster that money will come back to you.

There's no risk of a bill being "lost in the mail" either. As soon as you fax your document, you simply call your client and confirm that the fax arrived. If not, you can fax it again.

Faxing can also speed up your sales. Automobile dealers, for instance, shouldn't be without a fax machine in these tough times. What if you have a client who really wants to buy a new car, but who needs a credit approval to do so? You don't want to give that client a couple days to stew over his purchase—and possibly change his mind—while the credit application is mailed in, processed, and shipped back! With a fax machine, you can send, approve, and receive a credit application the same day. Your customer gets his car, and you get cash in the hand.

STRATEGY NUMBER 19: Use the Fax Machine to Speed Collections and Trim Expenses

HOW DOES THIS APPLY TO MY BUSINESS? _____

_____

_____

_____

_____

Priority   1   2   3   *(circle one)*   Action date _____

Potential dollar effect $ _____

Person assigned to this strategy _____

20. Double Check Scales for Accuracy

A little bit of waste—an ounce here, a gram there, a few pounds over there—may seem hardly worth worrying about when business is booming. But when the economy is in a nosedive and your company's future is at stake, eliminating every shred of waste becomes an important survival strategy.

Over time, scales do get out of kilter, and if left uncorrected, these inaccuracies can result in substantial losses to an organization. Just about every business incurs a certain amount of expense for postage, and some companies spend a considerable amount on it. With the price of first class postage now up to 29 cents an ounce, you could be wasting substantial resources if your scales are out of whack.

Indeed, if your company typically sends out thousands of pieces of mail and packages a year, an incorrectly calibrated scale that is off by only a fraction of an ounce can cost your company thousands of dollars in unnecessary postage expenses.

Here's a quick and easy way to test your postage scales for accuracy: dig out nine pennies from your pocket, and if they don't weigh in at one ounce, your weights are off. At businesses where raw materials are bought or sold in bulk, it's even more important to **regularly test the accuracy of all scales and other measuring instruments.**

If you're a baker and a slight miscalibration in your scale is causing you to use a bit too much flour or sugar in your products, you may not be able to taste the difference. But you may well feel the difference on your bottom line at the end of the year.

A manufacturer of brick and block found that his employees were using an extraordinary amount of sand and other raw materials. Indeed, the business's profit margins were razor thin because the cost of goods was so high in relation to the price the manufacturer was able to charge for finished products.

We suggested that management launch a concerted effort to reduce materials waste, starting with a check of all scales, and the implementation of new procedures for weighing all ingredients used in the manufacturing process.

By accurately weighing the raw materials and comparing that with the weight of the finished products, the company determined that almost 5 percent of the ingredients being used in the manufacturing process were wasted. If the company could eliminate even half that waste, the profitability of the business would rise at least 30 percent!

STRATEGY NUMBER 20: Double Check Scales for Accuracy

HOW DOES THIS APPLY TO MY BUSINESS? _____

_____

_____

_____

_____

Priority   1   2   3   *(circle one)*   Action date _____

Potential dollar effect $ _____

Person assigned to this strategy _____

21. Scale Back Your Orders—But Pounce on Deals

Statistically, it costs businesses an average of 2 percent a month to maintain inventory. When profits are slim, that's enough to eat a company alive! When times are tough, the general rule is to order merchandise only on an as-needed basis.

At the same time, however, remember that there are likely to be deals available in the marketplace that simply don't exist in a good economy. In dark times your suppliers are probably just as desperate as you are, and you may have opportunities to stock up on merchandise or supplies at bargain basement prices. The idea is to **keep your inventories tight so that you can cash in on opportunities** when they arise in the marketplace.

One distributor who followed this advice was able to cash in on a once-in-a-lifetime opportunity. The company distributes cleaning supplies and other products to the lodging industry, purchasing these items directly from various manufacturers.

Hard times set in, however, and the distributor encountered severe cash-flow problems. He went to one of his main suppliers and made the following proposition: he would agree to purchase all of his soaps and other cleaning supplies from this particular manufacturer in return for special terms that would help ease the company's cash-flow squeeze.

The supplier was experiencing problems of his own, and was only too happy to work out special terms in exchange for the security of the exclusive buying commitment offered by our client.

Under the arrangement they hammered out, as long as the distributor continued to purchase $100,000 in cleaning supplies from the manufacturer each month, he would not have to make payment until after it had been sold to the hotels.

Under this dating agreement, the distributor was effectively given a $100,000 interest-free permanent inventory advance that would never have to be paid for unless the company went out of business or its monthly orders dropped below the agreed-upon minimum.

In his books, the distributor recorded the advance as a debt—but it was a debt that never had to be paid back as long as the relation continued between the two parties.

Obviously, this was a great deal for him. The distributor's cash-flow problems dried up overnight. But it was also a terrific deal for the manufacturer, who gained a significant increase in sales and an assurance that this level of demand would continue over the years.

This particular arrangement was worked out almost ten years ago. Over that period, the distributor has never had to pay for his initial inventory, yet has turned that inventory over many times.

The manufacturer, in turn, is just as happy with the arrangement. The company has realized millions of dollars in extra sales volume over the years as a result of this exclusive purchase arrangement. And if the supplier never gets paid for that initial inventory shipment, he's made up that investment many times over in profits.

STRATEGY NUMBER 21: Scale Back Your Orders—But Pounce On Deals

HOW DOES THIS APPLY TO MY BUSINESS? _____

_____

_____

_____

_____

Priority   1   2   3   *(circle one)*   Action date _____

Potential dollar effect $ _____

Person assigned to this strategy _____

22. Negotiate Special Terms to Stretch Cash Flow

Someone once said that **everything** is negotiable. I don't know about that, but I do know that if your business regularly purchases substantial quantities of goods or services from another company, you're in a good position to negotiate favorable payment terms.

Particularly during periods of economic difficulty, your goal should be to **negotiate with suppliers for special terms that accommodate your cash flow requirements.** Indeed, whenever possible arrange to make payments **after** your busy season.

If you're a retailer and you generate a significant proportion of your sales during the holiday season, try to arrange for special dating that will allow you to pay for your merchandise after the end of the year. This is particularly true if you are in an inventory-intensive business.

A chain of jewelry stores buys merchandise throughout the summer and fall months in anticipation of a strong fourth quarter. The chain has been able to negotiate terms under which it is not required to pay for this merchandise until after the first of the year.

Given a choice, of course, any company would rather finance inventory with other people's money. But why would suppliers offer such terms? In many cases they are more than willing, in order to cement a long-term relationship with a good customer. It's certainly worth raising the issue with your sources of supply, particularly if you're in a position to increase your business with a company in return for better payment terms.

I know a distributor of seasonal goods who has this down to a science. In the winter months the company wholesales salt for use on the roads. In the spring they sell mulch, and in summertime they're into something else altogether. Because of cash flow considerations, the company makes it a point to negotiate payment terms that coincide with the nature of these seasonal operations. As a result, the distributor may receive a shipment of fertilizer in February, but won't be required to pay for it until May—after he has received payment from his customers.

The prize for negotiating favorable payment terms goes to a high volume auto parts distributor. This company worked out an arrangement with its principal supplier under which it agreed to substantially increase orders. In return, the manufacturer agreed to extend what amounts to a permanent $500,000 credit. Under their agreement, as long as the distributor's auto parts purchases remain above an agreed upon level, the $500,000 does not have to be repaid.

For example, if the distributor ordered parts totalling $1.2 million from the supplier, the amount payable to the supplier would only be $700,000.

The other $500,000 will never have to be paid unless, of course, the dealer switches suppliers or goes out of business. In this case, the distributor is enjoying free use of $500,000 worth of inventory. The parts manufacturer is effectively financing the wholesaler's operations in return for a commitment for continued business from that company.

STRATEGY NUMBER 22: Negotiate Special Terms to Stretch Cash Flow

HOW DOES THIS APPLY TO MY BUSINESS? _____

_____

_____

_____

_____

Priority   1   2   3   *(circle one)*   Action date _____

Potential dollar effect $ _____

Person assigned to this strategy _____

23. Trim the Cost of Credit Card Processing

Many businesses view credit cards as a necessary evil—"necessary" in industries where a large proportion of the customer pool expects them to be honored . . ."evil" because they can siphon off a substantial share of an organization's profits.

For their part, banks defend their credit card charges in light of their substantial processing costs. Imagine having to record and account for the information on all those barely legible slips of paper.

Banks have to charge for this processing, and depending on your volume of credit card business and the average size of each transaction, these charges can be prohibitive . . . as much as 5 percent, in some businesses.

Thanks to technology, however, there's a way to avoid such stiff charges. Instead of the old-fashioned credit card imprinter, for as little as $300 to $400 you can now buy an electronic charge device that will decode a customer's card and transmit the information automatically to the bank's computers. The proceeds can be transferred to your account literally overnight!

Best of all, by streamlining the bank's processing chores, **an electronic credit card device can cut your charge card fees in half!** These new "smart" credit card machines are really making converts out of businesses that have resisted charge cards in the past.

For example a very popular, successful restaurant stubbornly refused to honor credit cards for years. As the owner saw it, the business he lost by not accepting charges was offset by the bank fees he saved. The economics of the situation changed with the advent of the new electronic card machines, and he finally agreed to accept credit cards on a trial basis. It was one of the best moves he ever made!

The business's gross jumped from $14 million to just over $16 million, and by the end of a year the restaurant was realizing half of its total dollar volume from plastic. As an added bonus, internal theft—a big problem for the owner when the business was on a cash-only basis—dropped considerably.

Of course, the business did incur some additional expenses as a result of its acceptance of credit cards. At 1.5 percent, the processing fee charged by the banks for that $8 million in annual credit card volume amounted to $120,000.

But when you consider that the restaurant operated on a 33 percent gross profit margin, the additional $2.1 million generated by the acceptance of charge cards brought in $700,000 a year. Even after the $120,000 in processing costs, the restaurant was ahead of the game by $580,000 a year!

STRATEGY NUMBER 23: Trim the Cost of Credit Card Processing
HOW DOES THIS APPLY TO MY BUSINESS? _____

_____

_____

_____

_____

Priority   1   2   3   *(circle one)*   Action date _____

Potential dollar effect $ _____

Person assigned to this strategy _____

24. Avoid Costly Equipment Buying Blunders

Have you ever purchased new "state-of-the-art" equipment, only to discover that you paid dearly for those bells and whistles, yet could have managed nicely with a much more reasonably priced model?

Of course, the knife cuts both ways. It can be just as big a mistake to invest in a bargain basement piece of business equipment that can't do the job. You know the kind of gear I'm talking about. The stripped-down photocopy machine that doesn't collate documents the way you need them. The bottom-of-the-line fax machine that requires an employee to constantly hand-feed it. And, of course, last season's computer system that turns out to be incompatible with every other machine in the world!

In good times, these kinds of mistakes are embarrassing. In tough times they can be tragic.

A restaurant bought a $250,000 computer system that was intended to handle a variety of different accounting, inventory control, and internal management reporting functions. Unfortunately, however, the business didn't do its homework. The selection of the system was turned over to the restaurant's procurement chief—a fellow who was a whiz at finding the best quality prime beef and the lowest prices on Maine lobsters. Unfortunately, his expertise did not extend to computers.

The new quarter-million-dollar system arrived at the store in crates, the manufacturer offered virtually no set-up or training assistance, and it was a full year before the company was able to begin using the computer for its intended purposes. It was a horrible waste of time and money.

The correct way to select equipment for your business is to undertake a "needs" analysis examining your reasons for considering new gear, and the uses to which it will be put. Brainstorm with the people in your organization who will be using the equipment. Don't even think about shopping the market until it's clear to you what your company's needs are.

Once you've reached this point, begin comparing specifications systematically. Professional and industry associations often conduct tests of equipment, and trade publications are another potentially valuable source for product reviews.

If you're considering investing a significant sum in new equipment, ask the manufacturer or distributor for references from other companies in your line of business that have used this gear. Ask those references about the equipment's performance and reliability, and about the maintenance and repair service offered by the supplier.

If you do your homework, the right equipment choice should be obvious. If it isn't, maybe you should postpone the purchase, at least temporarily.

STRATEGY NUMBER 24: Avoid Costly Equipment Buying Blunders
HOW DOES THIS APPLY TO MY BUSINESS? _____

_____

_____

_____

_____

Priority   1   2   3   *(circle one)*   Action date _____

Potential dollar effect $ _____

Person assigned to this strategy _____

25. Review Spending for Publications and Organization Dues

At our house, we subscribe to a magazine we've been receiving for 27 years. We have probably looked at very few issues in the past ten years because our interests have changed. But that subscription form keeps coming in, and the magazine keeps getting renewed.

The same thing happens in business. There are magazines, journals, newsletters and other publications that companies receive, but nobody reads. Similarly, you may be paying dues to a trade association or other organization out of habit rather than because of the benefits of membership. Certainly, you must have had a good reason for joining the group or subscribing to the publication originally. But if they no longer serve a purpose, cut your losses.

I know of a real estate firm that subscribes to the *Federal Register*—a thick book of new rules and regulations published every business day by the government. The *Register* comes in every morning with the mail, and goes out unread every evening with the trash.

And we're not talking nickels and dimes, here. The *Federal Register* costs over $300 per year, an annual subscription to the *Wall Street Journal* will run you almost $150, and it's not unusual for industry newsletters to charge $500 or more per subscription.

The real problem is inertia. Subscriptions tend to continue to be renewed unless someone makes a conscious decision to cancel them. **Review your publication subscriptions and keep only those which continue to serve a purpose.**

Even if you decide to continue a publication, you may find that you can cut down on the number of copies you're paying for. At our firm we reduced the number of copies of the *Wall Street Journal* by 50 percent and now route them from desk to desk.

One business that I'm familiar with has come up with an especially creative way to reduce or eliminate publication costs. For years, this major chain of beauty shops spent upwards of $5,000 annually on magazines for customers to read under the hair dryers. Providing these publications was good business for the chain because it fostered goodwill among its clients. But it was also good business for the publishers of these magazines, because the publications received considerable exposure among the beauty shop patrons.

Recognizing this, the chain was able to approach the several leading publishers and negotiate free subscriptions for their shops—a maneuver that saved the chain hundreds of dollars every month.

Of course, your business may not be the type that would enable you to negotiate free subscriptions from publishers. But there are other ways that you may be able to trim your company's publication costs.

Start by giving one person in your organization responsibility for determining how many publications are being ordered on a monthly basis, and who is receiving them. Determine whether they offer any benefits to your firm, and whether several employees can share a subscription.

Give similar close scrutiny to membership dues that your company pays to various organizations. At our own office, for example, we've been paying some $500 each year in dues to provide membership for one of our employees in a local business organization. Our hope, of course, was that the individual would make contacts with area business people and ultimately attract new clients for the firm. When we discovered that our employee had stopped attending the group's meetings, we wasted no time in putting that $500 to better use.

Make sure that the benefits you reap from organization memberships and publication subscriptions exceed their cost. If employees want to order or continue receiving a particular publication, require that they explain in writing why this publication is important and how it will help them in their work. Ditto for organization memberships. If they're unable or unwilling to justify these expenditures, put your capital to better use.

EMPLOYEE ORGANIZATION CHECKLIST

Employee Name _____

Organization Name _____

Organization Address_____

_____

ANNUAL DUES _____

NUMBER OF MEETINGS/YEAR _____

NUMBER OF MEETINGS ATTENDED EACH YEAR _____

NAME(S), ADDRESSES, AND PHONE NUMBERS OF CONTACTS MADE THROUGH THE ORGANIZATION

1 _____

_____

2 _____

_____

_____

(Use additional paper if required)

PLEASE STATE YOUR GOALS VIS a VIS THIS ORGANIZATION FOR THE NEXT YEAR. (For example, the number of meetings you anticipate attending, the number of contacts you anticipate making, speeches or presentations that you plan to make, etc.)

_____

_____

_____

_____

Please sign here as an indication of your commitment to the above stated goals.

_____

STRATEGY NUMBER 25: Review Spending for Publications and Organization Dues
HOW DOES THIS APPLY TO MY BUSINESS? _____

_____

_____

_____

_____

Priority   1   2   3   *(circle one)*   Action date _____
Potential dollar effect $ _____
Person assigned to this strategy _____

26. Trim Back on Entertainment Expenses

Some people in business have managed to convince themselves that lavish forms of client entertainment are necessary to attract and retain customers. But even in the best of times, $100-a-plate lunches, corporate yachts, "skyboxes" at the Superbowl and similar extravagances are difficult to justify. When the economy isn't healthy, prodigal client entertainment practices can backfire on a company.

This isn't to say that client entertainment serves no valid business purpose, or that all expenditures in this area should be curtailed when business is down. In many industries, customer entertainment is an essential way to establish and cement a long-term relationship with a business associate.

Indeed, a business relationship without an element of customer entertainment is like a marriage without a courtship—it's clearly possible to carry it off, but it's likely to have some awkward moments.

The objective—particularly in a soft economy—is to use client entertainment to build a comfortable business relationship with your customers without going overboard. One approach being used by a number of companies today is to invite customers to a company picnic or outing. We've tried this at our firm with great success.

For some years now we've had a party for our staff at the end of tax season—sort of an April 15 victory celebration for our people each year at a farm in the country. We bring in a band and the farm serves us a barbecue dinner.

A few years ago we invited people who referred business to our firm to join us for the party. It was a big hit, and we were able to generate a lot of good will for our firm for only a little money. Since the band and the facilities were already paid for, the additional cost of bringing key business contacts to the affair averaged out to only about $15 a head for food and drinks.

Put on your thinking cap and I'll bet you can come up with some ideas for entertaining your clients without bankrupting the organization.

STRATEGY NUMBER 26: Trim Back on Entertainment Expenses
HOW DOES THIS APPLY TO MY BUSINESS? _____

_____

_____

_____

_____

Priority   1   2   3   *(circle one)*   Action date _____
Potential dollar effect $ _____
Person assigned to this strategy _____

27. Slash Your Paper Costs

For years now I've been reading about how computers, laser discs and other high tech electronic products are turning us into a "paperless society." At our office we have a computer on almost every desk, and we're as deeply committed to advanced technology as anybody. Yet it seems like we're using more paper in our business now than ever!

Like many firms, we've found that paper is a major expense item. In our business, client contact is essential, so every month we photocopy and distribute to each staff member an updated listing of the names, addresses and phone numbers of all our customers. We also churn out lots of internal memos, procedural manuals, and other printed material for our employees. On an annual basis, our company runs through several thousands of dollars worth of paper, just for our own internal use.

Recently, during a staff brainstorming session on ways to hold down our office operating costs, someone suggested a way we could **cut paper costs virtually in half by photocopying on both sides of the sheet.**

Admittedly, the savings aren't enough to allow us to buy a company yacht. But through this one simple, painless change in procedures, we've been able to increase our firm's bottom line by several hundred dollars each year.

More recently, we've started trimming our paper costs even further by shifting to lower priced recycled paper for internal use.

To be sure, the quality of recycled paper is several notches below top grade stock, and we don't use it for external communications to clients and business associates. But since it's available at up to 40 percent off the cost of regular paper, by using recycled stock for our internal needs, we're able to generate another couple hundred dollars for our year end profits—and help the environment at the same time! Every ton of recycled paper saves 7,000 gallons of water!

STRATEGY NUMBER 27: Slash Your Paper Costs
HOW DOES THIS APPLY TO MY BUSINESS? _____
_____
_____
_____
_____

Priority   1   2   3   *(circle one)*   Action date _____
Potential dollar effect $ _____
Person assigned to this strategy _____

28. Cancel Insurance on Unused Vehicles and Equipment

When business is off, many companies find themselves with a lot of vehicles or machinery that are not being used, particularly in the building trades and other industries vulnerable to seasonal or regular economic fluctuations.

On one hand, you don't want to get rid of the unused gear because you're probably going to need it when business picks up. On the other hand, you've got to economize to make it through the drought.

We often urge our clients to **trim expenses by dropping insurance coverage on idle equipment.** You would be surprised at the savings that can be realized.

One building contractor was nearly forced into early retirement when new construction activity in the area dried up. During a review of his operation he discovered that he had some 30 vehicles that were no longer being used. By cancelling insurance coverage on those vehicles, he saved at least $50,000 a year. When business perks up again, he will simply reinstate the insurance and drive off.

Similarly, if you have machinery or other equipment that is not being put to productive use, it may be possible to drop insurance on those items. The question to ask yourself is: would the loss or destruction of a particular piece of equipment create an economic hardship for you? If not, it may be a wise move to cancel coverage and pocket the insurance premiums.

A word of caution: before you drop the insurance, make sure that the equipment in question is not being used as collateral for a loan. Lenders usually require insurance coverage on items used as collateral. If you cancel the insurance, the lending institution may be able to declare you in violation of the loan agreement and demand full payment on the note.

And, before you drop the insurance on vehicles, check to find out whether your state will require you to turn in the license plates. If you must surrender your tags, your vehicles may have to be re-inspected before they can be re-licensed. If your vehicles are several years old, it could cost you far more to shape them up to pass inspection than you could possibly save in insurance costs.

STRATEGY NUMBER 28: Cancel Insurance on Unused Vehicles and Equipment

HOW DOES THIS APPLY TO MY BUSINESS? _____

_____

_____

_____

_____

Priority   1   2   3   *(circle one)*   Action date _____

Potential dollar effect $ _____

Person assigned to this strategy _____

29. Cash In on Tax Advantaged Employee Benefits

When business is down and profits are nonexistent, there may be very little money in the kitty for salary increases. Suppose, however, you found a way to offer your employees a significant pay raise, without using any of your money.

Impossible? Not at all! In fact, Uncle Sam will be happy to help you arrange this agreeable situation. And best of all, not only will your employees come out ahead, but your company will be money ahead as well!

The idea is to **offer your employees tax free fringe benefits in lieu of taxable wages.**

One of the smartest moves any employer can make is to set up a so-called "cafeteria plan" offering workers a selection of benefits that they can purchase with pre-tax dollars. These benefits may include child care, life and disability insurance, medical costs not covered by the employee's regular health insurance policy, health insurance premiums not paid by the company, and certain other items.

Under a cafeteria plan, employees are able to select a mix of benefits tailored to their individual needs and have the employer deduct the cost of those benefits from their salaries before they are taxed.

Suppose, for example, that Ms. X is in the 40 percent tax bracket for combined federal and state income taxes. If she spends $5,000 a year for childcare services and $1,000 annually on life insurance premiums, Ms. X will have to earn $10,000 in order to pay for those $6,000 in benefits.

If her employer adopts a cafeteria plan, however, Ms. X could elect to have $6000 deducted from her wages and earmarked for childcare and insurance costs. Right off the bat, the employee is $4,000 ahead because she didn't have to pay federal or state income tax on that money!

In addition, both Ms. X and her employer will realize a reduction in Social Security taxes. At the current rate of 7.65 percent, the Social Security tax saving on $6,000 comes to $459 for Ms. X and the same amount for her company.

There are some expenses involved for the employer: the cost of developing the plan, getting it approved by IRS, and administering it on a continuing basis. It has been our experience, however, that these costs are more than offset by the employers' savings due to lower Social Security tax and unemployment taxes.

If a company has 100 workers enrolled in such a plan, and they each contribute an average of $6,000 in pre-tax income, at 7.65 percent the employer's savings on Social Security taxes alone would total $45,900!

The real benefit, though, is to the employee. In our example, the employer was able to use cafeteria plan benefits to give Ms. X a "raise" of $4,459—and it didn't cost a plug nickel!

Another terrific employee program available to corporations is a 401K plan. Like an Individual Retirement Account, a 401K plan will allow employees to avoid income tax on part of their income which they save for retirement. Unlike an IRA, however, a 401K must be set up by the employer, and employees may be able to use it to tax shelter up to 15 percent of their gross income annually (up to a total of $8,475 in 1991).

An employee who earns $50,000 in income may contribute up to 15 percent—in this case, $7,500 each year. In effect, this 401K contribution reduces the individual's income from $50,000 to $42,500. If the employee's combined federal and state tax bracket is 40 percent, the individual winds up with $7,500 stashed away for retirement at a cost of only $4,500.

In effect, you've arranged for the government to give your employee a $3,000 raise!

STRATEGY NUMBER 29: Cash In on Tax Advantaged Employee Benefits

HOW DOES THIS APPLY TO MY BUSINESS? _____

_____

_____

_____

_____

Priority   1   2   3   *(circle one)*   Action date _____

Potential dollar effect $ _____

Person assigned to this strategy _____

30. Take Advantage of Local Seminars to Trim Travel Costs

It's tough having to break the news to your employees that profits are off and that they will have to suffer through some major belt-tightening for awhile. But it's even worse if your people don't believe you!

Let's say you've leveled with your staff, explained the financial plight of the company, and asked them to share in the sacrifices necessary to weather the economic storm. But then, while everyone is struggling to control costs, suppose the word gets out that one of your managers has taken off for Hawaii at company expense to attend a convention at a luxury resort!

How do you justify asking Tom and Dick to pinch pennies while Harry goes to the beach at Waikiki? Obviously, you don't. Even if attending the convention in Hawaii can be fully justified on business grounds, it may be unwise to do so when the business is facing hard times. Harry may well pick up some new clients at the meeting, but if you lose the confidence and cooperation of your staff, it won't be worth it!

Of course, if the meeting cannot be justified on business grounds, or if the payoff is at all questionable, then your decision is easy. Just don't go.

Consider the costs of sending people to an out-of-town convention or seminar. Start with at least $200 to $300 in air fare, $100 per night for hotels, another $50 per day in meals, plus several hundred dollars in registration fees. Add in cab fares, car rentals, telephone costs and all the other incidental expenses, and you'll find that it costs at least $2,000 to send each person to such a meeting.

As a more cost-effective alternative, consider sending people to seminars held locally, or perhaps even bringing the "seminar" to them. If you have a number of people in your organization who would benefit from participating in a certain meeting, consider bringing speakers in to meet with them rather than the other way around!

We've actually done that at our firm, and the savings are substantial. As with most other professions, accountants are required to undertake regular continuing professional education to retain their professional status. Our firm gladly pays for these courses because they help our people become more productive and effective professionals.

Currently, our accountants are obliged to attend 40 hours of continuing professional education annually, and it's not cheap. The required 40 hours of CPE instruction typically costs between $750 and $1,000, and the classes are often held at out-of-town locations. If you add in the cost of travel, hotels and meals, the tab comes to at least $2,000 per employee.

If you have, say, 20 professionals attending such meetings, you're looking at an expense in the neighborhood of $40,000 a year. And in a weak economy, that's not the kind of neighborhood you want to spend time in.

At our firm, we managed to trim those costs considerably by engaging professional speakers to come to our offices and hold seminars on the premises for our employees. We've found the cost to average about $400 a day per speaker. By bringing the experts to us, we've been able to reduce our firm's annual professional training and education costs from $40,000 to less than $5,000, without missing a beat!

Recently, we carried this concept a step farther by inviting other accounting firms in our area to send their professional people to our seminars—for a fee. It's a good deal for these other firms because they're able to reduce their CPE costs significantly, and it's an even better deal for us!

STRATEGY NUMBER 30: Take Advantage of Local Seminars to Trim Travel Costs

HOW DOES THIS APPLY TO MY BUSINESS? _____

_____

_____

_____

_____

Priority   1   2   3   *(circle one)*   Action date _____

Potential dollar effect $ _____

Person assigned to this strategy _____

31. Computer Monitor Your Company's Performance

This may sound like heresy coming from a CPA, but when you're forced to trim operating costs, expenditures for outside accounting services should come under review just like every other business cost. Fortunately, thanks to today's computer technology, it is possible for even small businesses to prepare a variety of performance management analyses internally.

To be sure, you'll still need an accounting firm to prepare your company's year-end financial statement. Indeed, your banker will probably insist on a review or audit of your figures by a CPA firm as a prerequisite for maintaining credit with the institution. But **any business that isn't using a computer to prepare its own monthly financial statements should start doing so immediately.**

That's just the beginning of how you can use your computer to get a better grip on the operation of your business. There are programs available that will allow you to track employee performance, measure sales per customer, monitor delivery times, and analyze literally thousands of other areas.

Even the smallest businesses with a very basic office PC can easily generate their own sophisticated management reports and reduce outside accounting fees considerably.

One of the most important tools available to businesses struggling to survive in a bad economy is an electronic spreadsheet program. (We use Lotus 1–2–3 at our firm and we think it's great!) With this software you can sort through your options by identifying the consequences of a variety of alternative actions. In effect, you can play a "what-if" game that will help you chart the best course for your business under various conditions.

We can take our bottom line projections for the quarter or the year and use this program to determine how profits will be affected by different factors. What if sales fall off 20 percent? What if interest rates rise? What if raw materials become unavailable? What if employee productivity increases?

Spread sheets are only one of the computer tools available to you. There are time management programs that can boost your organization's productivity, project management software to allow you to track the progress of various activities, and other programs that will help you do everything from control inventory to print employee newsletters.

These computer management tools are valuable to businesses anytime. During a recession, they might well provide the edge you need to ride out the hard times.

STRATEGY NUMBER 31: Computer Monitor Your Company's Performance

HOW DOES THIS APPLY TO MY BUSINESS? _____

_____

_____

_____

_____

Priority   1   2   3   *(circle one)*   Action date _____

Potential dollar effect $ _____

Person assigned to this strategy _____

32. Develop and Monitor Key Ratios for Your Business

When you're in battle for the survival of your business, you need reliable intelligence reports to marshal your defenses effectively.

Many companies are literally drowning in financial statistics and operating percentages. Don't just look at numbers on a balance sheet—find out what they truly mean. Your task is to sort through the financial information available to you and decide which variables are really important to the success of your operation.

In some respects, the most valuable way to express business information is in the form of a ratio: a shorthand expression of the relationship between two numbers. But because it enables you to convey a tremendous amount of information with a single number, a ratio can be a very powerful tool. Developing and maintaining **certain key ratios will allow you to monitor the pulse of your business.**

In order to develop meaningful ratios for your operations, you must not mix apples and oranges. If you're working with "income statement" items (i.e. income and expenses) for a quarter, then your "balance sheet" items (assets, liabilities and equity) should be *averaged* over that same three month period.

Ratios which are widely used by businesses today include:

•*Current Ratio*—The current assets of a business divided by current liabilities. This ratio is particularly meaningful to a short-term creditor, because it is a yardstick of the ability of the borrower to meet his current debts.

•*Acid Test Ratio*—The sum of a company's cash, marketable securities and net receivables divided by current liabilities. This figure, sometimes called the "quick ratio," measures the overall debt-paying ability of a business.

•*Advertising-to-Sales Ratio*—The company's total advertising expenditures divided by total sales. This figure will provide you with a warning signal if promotional costs are becoming excessive, or if advertising strategy is off target.

•*Equity Ratio*—Stockholders' equity divided by the sum of total liabilities plus stockholders' equity. This ratio is a measurement of the long-term solvency of a corporation. It is considered by many credit professionals as a key indication of credit strength of a business.

•*Daily Sales to Receivables Ratio*—Total trade accounts receivable divided by net sales on accounts, multiplied by 365. This figure provides an indication of how many days it takes your company to collect its receivables.

•*Inventory Turnover Ratio*—Total cost of sales divided by the average inventory on hand over the course of a year. This ratio is an important gage of profitability because it shows the number of times inventory turns during a business year.

Although ratios are useful in themselves—particularly if you compare them with the results from previous periods—they may be especially valuable as a device for evaluating your company's performance with those of others in your industry.

Many trade associations produce key ratio statistics, and you may also purchase surveys published by such firms as Dun and Bradstreet, and Robert Morris.

STRATEGY NUMBER 32: Develop and Monitor Key Ratios for Your Business

HOW DOES THIS APPLY TO MY BUSINESS? _____

_____

_____

_____

_____

Priority   1   2   3   *(circle one)*   Action date _____

Potential dollar effect $ _____

Person assigned to this strategy _____

33. Develop Regular Financial "Flash Reports"

Given a little advance warning, the captain of the Titanic could have avoided the iceberg. By the same token, many businesses at risk of going under in troubled economic waters can remain afloat if management obtains early warning of the dangers ahead.

In a poor economy, prudent business people generally do adopt a more cautious and defensive posture. But that's not enough. You need to **develop an early warning system within your organization that will alert you to problems in time to correct them.**

Too many business owners and managers make course corrections only four times a year—when the quarterly financial results are compiled. But waiting until the end of the quarter to identify problems within your company is like checking for icebergs once every few days.

I'm a firm believer in developing periodic "flash reports": up-to-the-minute snapshots of key financial information on the company's operations to supplement the regular financial statements. The information in this report should reflect the key financial variables in your particular business—items such as sales, payroll costs, billings, collections, travel expenses, and so forth.

There's no reason why a report like that can't be prepared for the owner or CEO by the 5th of every month during the accounting cycle. Indeed, for some businesses weekly or even daily flash reports would be worthwhile.

Armed with this early warning system, financial results will rarely come as a surprise to management. More importantly, if problems arise in sales, collections, production, payroll costs or other areas, they can be identified and addressed on a much more timely basis.

Although every business should develop and use a flash report, the data covered by these analyses should be tailored to your firm's specific operations. A flash report that would be valuable to a textile manufacturer would cover different items than one designed for an electrical contractor.

A law firm, for example, might develop a monthly flash report for the managing partner showing selected financial data for the previous month, including billings, collections, cash receipts, salaries and the number of new files opened. After a year or more of assembling these regular reports, the firm's comptroller will be able to provide the partners with historical trends. The lawyers can then compare last month's collections with those during the same period in the previous year.

A word of caution: it's tempting to go overboard and assemble monthly or weekly breakdowns of all kinds of financial data. If a flash report contains too much information, the key indicators of your company's health could get lost in the clutter.

As a rule of thumb, six key financial ratios should be enough to enable you to check the pulse of your business.

STRATEGY NUMBER 33: Develop Regular Financial Flash Reports
HOW DOES THIS APPLY TO MY BUSINESS? _____

_____

_____

_____

_____

Priority   1   2   3   *(circle one)*   Action date _____

Potential dollar effect $ _____

Person assigned to this strategy _____

Part II

External Cost Reduction

34. Watch Out for Unsound Banks

When a business goes under, the company's banker is sure to feel the impact. At best, the bank has lost a customer. Additionally, if the institution extended credit to the defunct business, some or all of that loan may have to be written off. If a number of businesses fold in response to a bad economy, the bank itself may be in jeopardy.

At our firm we recently pulled our funds out of an institution that used to be the largest bank in the state. During the past 12 months the bank's stock value dropped from $29 a share to $4 and it was clear that something was wrong. We did a little investigating, determined that the institution was indeed in trouble, and found a new place for our funds.

Many people believe that they have nothing to worry about as long as they stick to institutions insured by the Federal Deposit Insurance Corporation, and limit deposits to no more than $100,000 per account. In one sense, that is true.

Although there is talk now in Washington about changing the ground rules in the wake of the savings and loan mess, at this writing you could be sure that the government would stand behind you if you maintained no more than $100,000 in an FDIC-insured institution.

But even under the best of conditions, recovering your money from a failed bank or S&L can be a lengthy, frustrating and expensive process. Indeed, even if you're protected by a government-insured account, you may have to wait out in the cold for a long time to collect.

One advertising agency maintained a sizeable account in a state-insured S&L, and the owners of the business kept their personal funds there as well. Unfortunately, the institution collapsed without warning, and the agency's checks were bouncing all over town. When they tried to obtain their "insured" money, they found it was anything but a simple and quick procedure.

To be sure, they did recover their funds when their S&L was eventually taken over by another institution. However, they lost access to their money for almost two years, and they didn't earn a penny of interest on those funds for that entire period. It was a source of tremendous embarrassment and financial hardship for the owners of the business.

If you have reason to believe that your funds are in jeopardy, move to a safer bank.

Services such as Moodys and Standard & Poors publish credit ratings for publicly-held financial institutions. In addition, you can obtain a check on the credit worthiness of your bank over the phone through several organizations, including Veribanks in Wakefield, Mass. (800-44-BANKS). For a nominal fee, these outfits will provide you with a "safety rating" on any financial institution you name.

It's also important to verify the financial soundness of your insurance company. If there is a substantial claim against your business and your insurer lacks sufficient reserves to cover that claim, you could end up right behind them in bankruptcy court.

USA Today, as well as other publications, regularly report on the credit worthiness and soundness of insurance companies, and you can obtain credit ratings on these firms directly through both Standard & Poors and Moodys, as well as more specialized services such as A.M. Best (908–439–2200).

STRATEGY NUMBER 34: Watch Out for Unsound Banks
HOW DOES THIS APPLY TO MY BUSINESS? _____
_____
_____
_____
_____

Priority   1   2   3   *(circle one)*   Action date _____
Potential dollar effect $ _____
Person assigned to this strategy _____

35. Level With Your Banker about Financial Problems

When a major corporation is having a great year, the company is likely to churn out press releases announcing the results, and play up sales and earnings growth on the front page of the annual report.

But when the results are bad, you don't hear a peep from the management. It's human nature to keep bad news to yourself, I suppose. But ignoring a weak financial statement won't make it go away. If you know your business is having a bad year, then it's better to hash it out with the bank immediately.

Remember: bankers don't like surprises. If your company has an outstanding loan or line of credit at a bank, your banker may have gone to bat for you before the institution's loan committee. That won't happen again if he doesn't trust you.

In a weak economy, you just can't risk losing your bank's support. It should be standard operating procedure to **keep your banker posted on company finances—good or bad.** Indeed, it's good practice to send the bank interim statements and follow up with a phone call to avoid any misunderstandings down the road.

Too many businesses with bad financial reports often suffer from serious "bank-o-phobia." They're concerned that the banker will see only the bad news and none of the good. Often, however, these concerns are misplaced.

Recently, for example, we were able to work up a tremendous $5 million carryback-loss for a commercial construction company, only to have the owner thumb down our plan for fear of his banker's reaction. The principal was concerned that the carryback would weaken the firm's financial statement to the extent that the bank would limit his borrowing capacity.

With our client's permission I called his banker and explained the situation. In essence, I left the decision up to the bank. On the one hand, the company could forego the tax refund and present the lender with a very attractive financial statement. On the other hand, he could claim the tax loss and present a disastrous financial statement.

The bank pondered the situation for almost a week. They finally called back with instructions to go for the net operating loss carryback and forget about how the company would look on paper.

When the revised financial statements were prepared, they came as no surprise to the banker who was expecting a large loss. Our client's credit standing with his bank remained intact, and the owner pocketed a $1.7 million windfall from taxes he thought were paid and gone three years ago!

STRATEGY NUMBER 35: Level With Your Banker About Financial Problems

HOW DOES THIS APPLY TO MY BUSINESS? _____

_____

_____

_____

_____

Priority   1   2   3   *(circle one)*   Action date _____

Potential dollar effect $ _____

Person assigned to this strategy _____

36. Draw Up Contingency Financing Plans

In normal times, businesses typically arrange for financing through banks or other lending institutions. But when the wolf is at the door, bankers may be reluctant to sink any money into your company.

Don't kid yourself. Just because you play golf with the banker doesn't mean you will automatically get a loan when money is tight. Some of our clients have had long-term relations with banks and still were turned down cold when they desperately needed cash.

It's essential to **work up a rainy day action plan to secure financing from alternative sources.** Develop a "worst case scenario" for your company. What if sales dry up, production costs increase, collections fall off, the balloon payment comes due, and the bank won't lend you a dime?

Before all these terrible things happen, you need to develop a contingency plan for securing the funds necessary to save your business. For starters, consider the following options:

•*Arrange a Home Equity Line.* The same banker who won't lend you a red cent for your business may be happy to arrange a line of credit secured by the equity in your home. Set up such an equity line before you need it, keep it in reserve, and activate the line when you do need those rainy day funds.

•*Borrow from friends or family.* Aunt Sara or Uncle Joe may have substantial funds in a bank account or CD earning 7 percent. Assuming your business is basically sound, you would be doing them a favor by offering 11 percent or 12 percent on that money.

•*Tap corporate retirement plans.* You can't dip into your own company's employee pension funds, but you can borrow from the retirement plans of other businesses. Typically these plans are loaded with cash, and much of it is in low-yield, highly liquid investments. To be sure, the trustees of a corporate retirement plan have a fiduciary responsibility to invest these funds prudently. But as long as your company is profitable and has equity on the balance sheet, you may be an ideal candidate to secure financing from another business's pension plan.

•*Sell off assets.* One of our clients collected high-quality antiques which had appreciated in value considerably over the years. When business fell off, the owner was able to raise significant cash to reinvest in the company by auctioning off those valuable antiques.

•*Collateralize assets.* Even in bad times, bankers are often willing to lend money to a struggling business that is willing to offer its inventory or accounts receivable as collateral. Asset-based financing is a promising way to raise money even if your financial statement is weak.

•*Factor accounts receivable.* If all else fails, you may be able to raise cash from a lender willing to advance you a percentage of your receivables. Factoring receivables is a relatively expensive source of financing, and in a sense you may be mortgaging the future of your business. But desperate times call for desperate actions.

•*Enlist a financial broker.* For a fee, such an individual will counsel you on securing financing, assist you in putting together a proposal, and even negotiate the terms of the loan on your behalf. Having a broker handle these arrangements often eliminates emotional complications that interfere with effective negotiations. Expect to pay a financial broker either a fixed fee that's contingent on obtaining a loan, or a percentage of the amount financed.

STRATEGY NUMBER 36: Draw Up Contingency Financing Plans

HOW DOES THIS APPLY TO MY BUSINESS? _____

_____

_____

_____

_____

Priority   1   2   3   *(circle one)*   Action date _____

Potential dollar effect $ _____

Person assigned to this strategy _____

37. "Lease" Your Employees to Other Businesses

One of the toughest things about a business downturn is having to lay off people who contributed to the success of your company during the good times. It's one thing to fire an individual for not doing a good job, and quite another to have to discharge a productive and trusted employee.

Aside from the very difficult emotional aspects, there are business implications that must also be weighed. When you're forced to let a valued employee leave your organization during a business slump, you've lost all the time, energy and expertise that you've invested in that person over the years.

When the economy turns around and business picks up, you may have to start all over and make a similar investment in a new employee. Worse yet, the valued associate whom you terminated might well return to haunt you by taking a job with one of your competitors!

Needless to say, firing good employees should be a last resort. Even if there's not enough business coming in to keep your people busy, there are ways to keep valued employees on the payroll.

One technique is to **"lease" out idle employees to other businesses.** In effect, your company acts as a temporary employment service. This way you can keep your employees on staff, and make some money, to boot.

Virtually every type of business could use this technique to subsidize payroll costs. If your employees are valuable to you, they are almost certain to be valuable to others, as well. A commercial construction company, for example, could temporarily "lease" a foreman or surveyor to a residential builder. Company collection managers, accountants, secretaries could all be "rented" to other businesses for a few days a week, or a few hours a day. You never know who needs good, part-time help—maybe even the office down the hall.

I've known companies to go so far as to donate the services of their employees to charity in order to keep them on the payroll. When the housing market collapsed, a home construction company had virtually no business, and even less need for a comptroller. Instead of letting this individual go, his employer continued to pay his salary. In return, the comptroller donated his time and expertise to a charity organization that builds camps for needy children.

The contractor, of course, didn't make any money on this deal. But it generated an enormous amount of good will for the company, and it kept a valued employee in the stable until the market bounced back.

STRATEGY NUMBER 37: "Lease" Your Employees to Other Businesses

HOW DOES THIS APPLY TO MY BUSINESS? _____

_____

_____

_____

_____

Priority   1   2   3   *(circle one)*   Action date _____

Potential dollar effect $ _____

Person assigned to this strategy _____

38. Comparison Shop Banks to Lower Credit Card Fees

When cash is tight, you wouldn't buy a car from a dealer who charges $5,000 above the sticker price, and you certainly wouldn't go out of your way to shop at a store where the prices are 50 percent higher than everywhere else.

But you would be surprised at how many otherwise prudent businessmen squander company money by paying excessive credit card processing fees. Often this is because they don't realize that **different banks impose different charges for processing charge card transactions, and it pays to shop for the best deal.**

Credit card processing fees are determined by a number of variables, including:

1. The number of transactions;
2. The dollar amount of those transactions;
3. The type of equipment used; and
4. Your ability to negotiate fees with the bank.

Depending on these factors and on the card that is used, processing fees can range anywhere from a low of 1–1/2 percent to more than 5 percent. If someone's raking 5 percent off the top, they're actually taking a considerable chunk off your bottom line. At more than a few firms, these credit card fees are the deciding factor in whether the company enjoys a profit or slips into the red.

Fortunately, there are ways to trim these costs.

One is to encourage cash payments by setting a high dollar minimum for all credit card sales. Some establishments set the threshold as high as $25 per transaction. Although you may lose some sales if you set the purchase minimum too high, you'll never know unless you try.

Another, even better way of slashing these expenses is to negotiate a processing fee reduction with your bank.

One of our clients operates a popular, upscale restaurant where the check average is well over $50, and much of the business is done by credit card. At our suggestion, the restaurant scrapped its old credit card imprinters and invested in state-of-the-art electronic credit card processors.

These new card processors cost the restaurant less than $300 apiece, but it was the best investment that business ever made. Because the new equipment significantly reduced the cost of processing transactions at the bank, the bank was able to lower the fee charged to the restaurant by 1–1/2 percent.

Now, 1–1/2 percent may sound like small potatoes, but it isn't. This particular restaurant does $20 million annually in credit card transactions. The processing fee reduction saved the company $300,000 a year!

STRATEGY NUMBER 38: Comparison Shop Banks to Lower Credit Card Fees

HOW DOES THIS APPLY TO MY BUSINESS? _____

_____

_____

_____

Priority   1   2   3   *(circle one)*   Action date _____

Potential dollar effect $ _____

Person assigned to this strategy _____

39. Use a "Dunning Service" to Avoid Collection Agency Fees

The difficulties that many companies encounter during an economic downturn are not due to a drop in business, but to a decline in collections. When money is tight, your customers are likely to have trouble paying their bills. Your objective should be to convince them that your bill deserves priority attention.

When in-house collection efforts fail, most business people swallow hard and turn their past-due accounts over to a collection agency. That should be a last gasp alternative, because most collection agents will keep anywhere from 25 percent to 33 percent or more of whatever they are able to recover from your customers.

Before turning unpaid bills over to a collection agent, you should **consider using a computerized "dunning service" to recover payment.** Unlike a collection agency, these services take no action to recover the debt other than to send out letters. But the letters they send are extremely official looking documents designed to grab attention. If someone brought 100 pieces of mail to your desk, theirs would be the one you would open first.

One service offers a choice of letters ranging from a "diplomatic" message to a pretty tough one. The dunning agent sends out up to eight of these letters over a 12 week period to each account you designate, and every subsequent letter is a little stronger than the last one.

When the customer settles up or commits to a repayment schedule, you simply notify the dunning service and the letters stop. If the customer doesn't follow through on the agreement, you can contact the service and the computers start spitting out dunning notices again.

Believe it or not, this approach is extremely effective—and extremely cost effective. We use a nationally franchised dunning service with branches in many major markets—and they claim an average payment rate of 59 percent. For some of our clients, the collection rate has been even higher.

The cost of this service runs only about $9 per account. You couldn't send out eight letters yourself for that! And when you consider that the alternative is a collection agency that may keep a third of what they recover, a dunning service is an even bigger bargain.

Suppose you have 50 customers behind in payments to you. Despite your own letters and phone calls, these accounts are still in arrears by an average of $500 each. If you go to a dunning service and their computer-generated letters result in payments by half of those accounts, it has cost you about $450 (50 x $9) to recover $12,500.

If you had turned these accounts over to a collection agency, it would have cost you over $3,000 to recover these same payments.

Admittedly, a dunning service isn't going to bat 1000 for you. But the accounts that don't respond to these letters can then be turned over to the collection agency as a true last resort.

CLIENTS SENT TO COLLECTIONS
PERIOD ENDING _____

CLIENT NAME	AMOUNT DUE	DUNNING SERVICE	COLLECTION SERVICE	ATTORNEY

STRATEGY NUMBER 39: Use a "Dunning Service" to Avoid Collection Agency Fees

HOW DOES THIS APPLY TO MY BUSINESS? _____

_____

_____

_____

_____

Priority   1   2   3   *(circle one)*   Action date _____

Potential dollar effect $ _____

Person assigned to this strategy _____

40. Hire a Collection Manager or Agency to Boost Cash Flow

Lethargic collection practices are absolute poison to a business struggling in a soft economy.

Unfortunately, collections are treated as the company stepchild in many organizations. It's an unpleasant chore that people would rather put off doing, or delegate to somebody else.

This is a shame because at many companies **the shortest route back to the black is to recover overdue accounts receivable.** If your cash flow is suffering because of overdue accounts, it's time to consider either an outside agency or an in-house collections manager to speed up payments.

Be careful, however. Not everybody is cut out to be a good collections agent. Whether you bring in an outside specialist or assign the job to an existing employee, it's important to choose someone with the right personality and temperament. The ideal person is friendly but firm, tough but not offensive—and if you find the right individual, the payoff will be substantial. Indeed, a good collections manager can generate more cash for your firm in an hour than a salesman can produce in a week!

At our own firm we practice what we preach. We recently took a close look at our accounts receivables and discovered a disturbing trend toward overdue accounts. We hired a full-time collections manager who began paying dividends right from the start.

During the first eight weeks our new collections manager was able to clean up 20 percent of the receivables that had been overdue by 60 days or more. That income alone was enough to pay our new manager's salary for years!

As an alternative to appointing a full-time collections chief, many businesses have experienced success by paying their salespeople commissions based on the company's collections.

This way the sales staff is motivated to collect payment as well as make a sale. When one of our clients switched to this approach, the average age of his accounts receivables dropped by 30 days!

The end result was that our client was able to reduce his business debt by 50 percent, and save tens of thousands of dollars in interest each year.

STRATEGY NUMBER 40: Hire a Collection Manager or Agency to Boost Cash Flow

HOW DOES THIS APPLY TO MY BUSINESS? _____

_____

_____

_____

_____

Priority   1   2   3   *(circle one)*   Action date _____

Potential dollar effect $ _____

Person assigned to this strategy _____

41. Pick Your Insurance Agent's Brains to Trim Premiums—Part I

A recent survey found that at the average company today, the cost of employer-provided health insurance is equivalent to 26 percent of net earnings. On an annual basis, the cost of health care is now averaging more than $3,200 per worker. That's a heavy load in the best of times. In a sick economy, the burden of providing increasingly costly health insurance coverage may be enough to pull the entire company under.

Sit down with your insurance agents and explore options for reducing the cost of coverage.

One approach that a number of businesses have tried is to freeze the company's contribution toward employee health insurance. If you're paying out, say, $200 per month toward each worker's health coverage, you could agree to continue that same dollar contribution next year. But any premiums above this amount would have to be paid by the employee.

To help workers deal with future increases in premium costs, many employers now **offer lower cost coverage options such as a health maintenance organization or a preferred provider organization.**

Similarly, talk with your agent about ways to reduce the cost of other types of insurance.

Disability coverage, for example, is extremely important —it's the family's safety net if the breadwinner becomes incapacitated. But when cash is short, it may be difficult to pay the premiums. Instead of letting coverage lapse and losing this protection, consider reducing premium costs by accepting a longer "elimination period."

Many disability insurance policies don't begin paying benefits until you've been incapacitated for 30 days. By switching to an elimination period of 60, 90 or even 180 days you can maintain the same dollar coverage and significantly lower your premium costs.

Your agent may also be able to help you achieve substantial savings on life insurance costs by putting your dividends to work to offset your premiums. That could be the next best thing to "free" life insurance!

STRATEGY NUMBER 41: Pick Your Insurance Agent's Brains to Trim Premiums—Part I

HOW DOES THIS APPLY TO MY BUSINESS? _____

_____

_____

_____

_____

Priority   1   2   3   *(circle one)*   Action date _____

Potential dollar effect $ _____

Person assigned to this strategy _____

42. Pick Your Insurance Agent's Brains to Trim Premiums—Part II

Being underinsured can be risky for a business. But by the same token, being overinsured can impose significant unnecessary costs on a company. You would be surprised at the number of businesses that waste considerable sums of money because they have duplicative, unnecessary or obsolete insurance coverage.

Take motor vehicle insurance. Some people insure business as well as personal vehicles under policies calling for a $100 or $200 deductible. But this often makes no sense.

Of course, businesses need insurance as a hedge against major losses—you don't need protection against damages amounting to a few hundred dollars. If a company car or truck is damaged in an accident, it isn't likely to be much of a hardship for the business to absorb the first $500 or $1,000 in repairs. So why not raise the deductible on your company's policy to $500 or $1,000?

Sit down with your insurance agent and have him crunch the numbers for you. You'll be surprised at how much lower your annual premiums will be if you raise deductibles.

Don't limit your focus to automobile insurance, however. **Ask your agent for suggestions on how to trim other insurance costs, as well.** There are ways to reduce premiums for all types of coverage—it just takes a little creative brainstorming.

A commercial glass distributor, for example, was encountering steep Workman's Compensation premiums due to the heavy number of claims being filed by her employees. It wasn't that the company was out of compliance with workplace safety requirements, or that the employees were particularly accident prone. The high level of claims was a reflection of the nature of our client's business.

But while the distributor couldn't cut down on the injury rate, she could take steps to reduce the number of Workman's Comp claims filed by her people. The company contracted with a nearby medical clinic to treat employees with minor bruises, cuts, strains and other injuries for a flat monthly retainer.

Because the clinic arrangement sharply reduced the incidence of Workman's Comp claims by employees, the company's premiums dropped equally sharply. After a while she ran a comparative cost analysis and found that for every dollar she paid to this medical clinic, the company saved $2 in insurance premiums.

When you review your company's Workman's Comp costs, it's important to examine the risk categories to which your employees are assigned. The drivers for a trucking company that specializes in delivering explosives would likely be rated high-risk employees. But those high rates should not apply to the company's dispatcher, bookkeeper or secretary.

It's in your interest to convince your insurance agent to place each of your workers in the lowest risk class possible.

STRATEGY NUMBER 42: Pick Your Insurance Agent's Brains to Trim Premiums—Part II
HOW DOES THIS APPLY TO MY BUSINESS? _____

_____

_____

_____

_____

Priority   1   2   3   *(circle one)*   Action date _____
Potential dollar effect $ _____
Person assigned to this strategy _____

43. Form Your Own "Kitchen Cabinet" of Business Advisors

Nobody has all the answers, and in a difficult economy your company's future may very well depend on the quality of advice you receive from others.

To be sure, courses in business management and books like this one can help you chart a course that can keep your company afloat. But they're no substitute for input from knowledgeable people familiar with your organization's strengths and weaknesses.

Assemble a small group of trusted advisors, such as your attorney, the CPA, the banker, and insurance agent for a meeting with your top management perhaps once every three months. Set a clear agenda for the meeting. Talk with them about sales, about profitability, about operating costs, about reducing the risks that your company faces in troubled times. You'll be astonished at the ideas that can come out of these kinds of meetings.

Too many people in business tend to view their outside resources as one-dimensional. The lawyer is somebody to talk to only when there is a contract to draft or litigation to discuss. The accountant is just an historical record keeper who helps you develop financial statements and tax forms. A banker is someone you see for financing. And so on.

If this is how you view these resources, you're missing the boat. As an accountant myself, I can tell you that the services provided by your CPA should not cost your business a red cent! Every penny that you pay to your accountant should come back to you, with interest, through improvements in your operation. Similarly, your attorney, your accountant, your insurance agent, your advertising agency—these all can and should be profit centers for your firm. There's no reason to look at these people as dead costs.

It's up to you to make it clear that you expect them to come up with advice that will help your company increase sales, or reduce costs, or expand markets, or improve in some other way. If they can't help you in this respect, rethink your relationship with them.

STRATEGY NUMBER 43: Form Your Own "Kitchen Cabinet" of Business Advisors

HOW DOES THIS APPLY TO MY BUSINESS? _____

_____

_____

_____

_____

Priority   1   2   3   *(circle one)*   Action date _____

Potential dollar effect $ _____

Person assigned to this strategy _____

44. Farm Out Payroll Chores to an Outside Automated Service

Many businesses spend a tremendous amount of valuable staff time and effort computing payrolls, calculating withholding taxes, and figuring health insurance deductions for every employee. As a rule of thumb, **if you have more than 15 employees, you're probably money-ahead to use an outside payroll service.**

Typically, these services are highly automated and are able to make corresponding entries on a payroll check, ledger and employee pay stub. From this information, the service can generate year-end payroll reports, produce W-2s for all your employees, and provide you with other valuable management information.

Most of these automated services will be able to handle your payrolls regardless of whether your employees are paid a salary, on an hourly basis, by commission, or whatever. Many are set up so that you can phone in payroll information to them, and they will then calculate each worker's check and deliver them to you on payday.

These automated services can even increase staff productivity by providing electronic payroll check deposits directly into each employee's checking account. If you figure that the typical employee spends an average of 15 minutes out of the workday to deposit each paycheck, and there are 24 paydays a year, a direct deposit payroll system can boost your organization's productivity by one full workday per employee per year!

Best of all, these services are relatively inexpensive. For many companies the cost works out to as little as $1 per employee per pay period. If you're running a business with 50 employees, spending $50 or so for a payroll is a real bargain.

There are lots of payroll services available to you, including some national organizations such as ADP (Automatic Data Processing) and Paychex. Finding the right one for your company requires some research on your part, however. Trade publications and professional association journals often carry ads for payroll services that specialize in your type of business. Or, ask your accountant to recommend one that has been used successfully by some of his other clients.

Even if your organization is smaller, it's frequently worthwhile to consider using a commercial payroll service.

Indeed, even if an outside service doesn't save you a dime, it may offer other valuable benefits, including:

- Enhanced payroll confidentiality (fewer people in your organization will have access to this information);

- Insulation against late payroll tax filings and the IRS penalties they can produce;
- Relief from constantly having to track and adjust to changes in local, state and national payroll tax ground rules;
- Availability of customized, comprehensive and easy-to-read management reports on payroll records.

STRATEGY NUMBER 44: Farm Out Payroll Chores to an Outside Automated Service

HOW DOES THIS APPLY TO MY BUSINESS? _____

_____

_____

_____

_____

Priority   1   2   3   *(circle one)*   Action date _____

Potential dollar effect $ _____

Person assigned to this strategy _____

45. Tap Outside Investors for Capital

The first stop for most business owners in need of fresh capital is the local bank. But banks, S&Ls and other **financial institutions aren't the only source of funds for businesses, and often they're not the best source.** Indeed, many successful entrepreneurs regard banks as the "last resort"—the place to go for financing when all other options fail.

In a chilly economic climate, business owners seeking capital would be particularly wise to remember this. Financial institutions become very reluctant to lend money during a business downturn.

From your perspective, there may be little or no risk at all associated with the loan. The extra capital will enable you to add new facilities, expand existing ones, broaden your market share, and pole-vault your company to a new plateau of profitability. But convincing a gun-shy banker of these truths may prove a difficult task.

A successful real estate investor, with a number of valuable properties and a net worth of nearly $20 million, wanted to remodel one of her facilities and sought to borrow $350,000 for this purpose. As collateral, she was willing to put up a piece of real estate appraised at more than $1 million. Clearly, here was a loan proposition safe as Gibraltar. Yet she was turned down flat by the bank! She visited three other institutions, and it was the same story. Because of the general economic situation, the banks were all simply refusing to consider any financing arrangements involving commercial real estate.

In the end, the investor did what some say businesses should do in the first place: she arranged to finance her remodeling program through outside investors.

Finding private investors willing to bankroll a sound business project isn't as difficult as it may sound, even in a weak economy. There are plenty of people who have pulled their money out of real estate or the stock market, and these individuals are looking for a safe place to invest those funds at attractive rates.

Squirreling money away in a bank or in T-bills will yield them, maybe, 8 percent. By offering them the equivalent of the interest rates charged by commercial lenders, say 12 percent or so, you've enabled them to increase their yield by 50 percent—an extremely attractive proposition for any private investor.

To be sure, you're not likely to attract any investors if you're seeking capital merely to keep a foundering business afloat for a few more months. But if your company is sound to begin with and an influx of fresh funds would make it even stronger, then you're a prime candidate for outside investors.

One of the most frequently overlooked sources of outside capital is the money sitting around in employee retirement plans. To be sure, your company can't borrow from the pension fund set up on behalf of your employees. But other companies can tap into your retirement program for financing. And by the same token, your business can borrow from the pension funds set up by other companies.

A corporate retirement fund earning 8 percent or 9 percent on its money would likely be very interested in bankrolling a sound investment in your company that would yield, say, 12 percent or 13 percent.

Another excellent source of outside capital is your own circle of friends. Assuming the investment truly is rock solid, you'll be doing friends or family a favor by offering them a high rate of return on their funds.

If you do borrow from friends or family, though, keep it as an arms-length transaction. Offer them the same collateral that you would give to a bank—a mortgage on the property, corporate guarantees, personal guarantees, and so on.

STRATEGY NUMBER 45: Tap Outside Investors for Capital
HOW DOES THIS APPLY TO MY BUSINESS? _____

_____

_____

_____

_____

Priority   1   2   3   *(circle one)*   Action date _____

Potential dollar effect $ _____

Person assigned to this strategy _____

46. Renegotiate Your Lease to Reduce Occupancy Costs

When the economy catches cold, the commercial real estate market goes into double pneumonia. Office building owners and other commercial landlords become desperate for tenants and they're often willing to offer low rates and lucrative concessions to attract them.

It wouldn't be surprising to learn that some of the newer businesses in your building are paying considerably less rent per square foot than you are. Even though you may have been one of the landlord's oldest and most valued tenants, the newcomers who came aboard in a bad economy are likely to be receiving far more favorable treatment.

The advice that I give to our clients is to approach the landlord and suggest that it may be in their mutual interest to renegotiate the existing lease arrangement.

A business tenant who has made rent payments consistently and absorbed rent increases over the years should not hesitate to **suggest that the landlord lower the rent to reflect current market conditions.** As an alternative, some business owners have negotiated a temporary rent deferral or reduction in lease payments to help them through the hard times.

In return, you might indicate that you're willing to commit to a longer lease period as part of the renegotiation. Of course, the landlord could turn you down flat. But if your occupancy costs truly are above the market, the building owner will recognize that if he refuses to deal with you now, he will risk losing all rental income on the space when your current lease is up. If you only have a year or two remaining on your present lease and you're able to commit now to an additional five year extension, a reasonable landlord will think long and hard before turning down your proposal for a rent rollback.

A Washington lobbying firm has leased extensive office space for years in one of the city's most prestigious buildings. When the economy softened and the firm's cash flow became tight, they approached the building owner.

The meeting lasted about three minutes. The landlord immediately offered to trim the rent by one-third, and the lobbyists jumped at the deal because it eased their tight cash situation considerably.

But it was a good move from the landlord's point of view, as well. As he saw it, it was better to have two-thirds of the rent in his pocket than to be owed 100 percent of the rent by a tenant who might never be able to pay it.

While existing tenants have some extra leverage in negotiating with landlords during a poor economy, businesses shopping for new space to rent are really in the driver's seat. There truly are some incredible opportunities available to companies willing and able to make long term commitments during a recession.

A printer who lost his existing location due to an urban renewal project found a 13,000 square foot facility that the building owners were extremely anxious to rent. He agreed to a ten-year lease, and in return the landlord picked up all of his moving expenses and paid the printer $1.2 million in cash, up front. That might have been the deal of the century!

STRATEGY NUMBER 46: Renegotiate Your Lease to Reduce Occupancy Costs

HOW DOES THIS APPLY TO MY BUSINESS? _____

_____

_____

_____

_____

Priority   1   2   3   *(circle one)*   Action date _____

Potential dollar effect $ _____

Person assigned to this strategy _____

47. Schedule a Year End Tax Planning Session With Your CPA

It's never a good time to pay too much in taxes. But when you're fighting for the survival of your company, it's a crying shame to overpay the IRS. There are ways for businesses to reduce their tax burden that aren't illegal, immoral or fattening. But it takes some creative planning before the end of the fiscal year. Little, if anything, can be done after the tax year ends.

Meet with your accountant two months before the end of the year to do tax planning and prepare an annual tax projection. The idea is to **shift income and expenses from one year to another to ease the tax bite.**

If it turns out you are doing OK this year but expect a significant falloff in earnings the next year, your accountant can suggest a number of ways to reduce the overall tax burden by absorbing expenses in the profitable year, or postponing income until the bad year.

Among other things, businesses can pay employee bonuses early; stockpile supplies for the coming year; donate slow-moving merchandise to charity before year end; or claim a tax loss by disposing of unused assets early.

If the situation is the opposite—you expect recovery in the coming months after a downturn in the current year—simply reverse the process and reduce next year's taxable income.

A creative accountant can also help you avoid certain kinds of year-end financial transactions that could have severe negative tax implications for your business and your family.

During a year-end planning session with one of our new clients we learned that the business owner was refinancing his home to raise $100,000 to repay money that he had borrowed from his own Subchapter S Corporation. We convinced him that this would be a costly and unnecessary maneuver.

Instead, we suggested that he have the corporation pay him a $100,000 bonus, which he would immediately pay back to the corporation to eliminate the debt. Because he was the sole stockholder in the company, there was no tax effect.

Granted, the reason this maneuver worked was that our client had structured his business as a Subchapter S Corporation—an arrangement that allows corporate tax benefits such as the $100,000 deduction to flow directly to the shareholder.

The moment the corporation paid him the $100,000 bonus, his personal taxable income rose by that amount. The fact that he immediately paid that money back to the company to eliminate the loan did not relieve him of his personal tax liability. But by paying the owner that year-end bonus, the Corporation earned itself a $100,000 tax deduction. And since it was an "S" corporation, the company's deduction filtered through directly to the shareholder—our client—who used that $100,000 deduction to offset his extra $100,000 of income. For tax purposes, it was a wash!

The bottom line is that our client did not have to refinance his home, the corporation retained all of its cash, the owner's debt was wiped off the books, and there were no income taxes to pay on the entire transaction.

STRATEGY NUMBER 47: Schedule a Year End Tax Planning Session with Your CPA
HOW DOES THIS APPLY TO MY BUSINESS? _____
_____
_____
_____
_____

Priority   1   2   3   *(circle one)*   Action date _____
Potential dollar effect $ _____
Person assigned to this strategy _____

Part III

Asset and Credit Management

48. Tighten Up Credit Practices

Poor credit policies are a prescription for trouble any time. In a slack economy, they're poison.

It's not unusual during an economic downturn for customers to become sluggish about paying creditors. The 30-day account becomes a 60-day account, or maybe even a 90- or 120-day account.

Too often, businesses without proper credit procedures find themselves in deep trouble without warning. You can avoid such unpleasant surprises by keeping close tabs on the customers to whom you extend credit. If a customer who has always paid promptly suddenly begins paying more slowly, it can be an important danger signal. Contact that customer immediately and let them know your concerns. Then go to work shoring up your company's credit policies.

Here's how:

1. **Assign a due date to all bills.** You've got to remind customers of your credit terms. Check the invoices and/or statements you send out to make sure your customers are clearly informed of what is expected from them. Do they explain whether payment is due upon invoice rendered? Or within 30 days? We reviewed the billing practices of our new clients, and we found that almost half of them fail to include specific payment terms on

their statements. They might as well be asking customers to pay late! After all, if a customer receives two bills, and one says "Net 30" and the other says nothing, you can be sure which one will go on the back burner.

2. Offer discounts to early payers. Don't overlook any opportunity to accelerate your cash flow. You should even consider offering your customers discounts of 1 percent to 2 percent if bills are paid within 10 days of delivery. It may cost you a little, but it may also light a fire under slow payers—and that could have a major effect on your cash flow.

3. Telephone tardy customers. It's one thing to get a letter in the mail warning you that your bill is past due; it's another to hear it over the phone from a collections manager! If your customers are behind on their payments, get on the horn and let them know it. Not only are you alerting them that you are concerned, but you're verifying that the bill actually arrived.

4. Require customers to sign a statement of contract. A written agreement at the onset of a business relationship can help you avoid misunderstandings later in the game. Spell out the terms of the arrangement on your credit application form so they are clear from the start. You might want to go one step farther and have customers sign a separate credit statement or contract identifying not only when payment will be due, but also that the customer is liable for any legal or arbitration costs should the bill not be paid. Many businesses already use a standard credit contract: a form they can photocopy and use for almost any transaction. However, if you're considering an especially important deal, you might want to draw up a more explicit contract with your attorneys.

5. File a security agreement at the courthouse. If you're especially nervous about a particular customer coming through on a deal, consider a security agreement. This type of arrangement entitles you to first claim on any goods you've shipped. If the customer doesn't pay for the goods, you can recover your shipment. Even if the customer goes bankrupt, your goods will not be subject to the general claims of other creditors.

6. Stop goods and/or services. The last and most drastic option for creditors is to stop shipments or withhold services from non-paying clients. Nobody wants to lose customers—especially not during periods when business is tough to come by. But in a recession there are some companies that switch from supplier to supplier leaving a trail of unpaid bills and disappointed vendors. If you don't get your money, don't hesitate to stop a transaction. It pays to play it safe.

STRATEGY NUMBER 48: Tighten Up Credit Practices
HOW DOES THIS APPLY TO MY BUSINESS? _____

_____

_____

_____

_____

Priority   1   2   3   *(circle one)*   Action date _____
Potential dollar effect $ _____
Person assigned to this strategy _____

49. Check References Before Extending Credit to a New Customer

Bringing in a new customer is always exciting, and it's doubly so in tough economic times. But don't get carried away. It's one thing to make a sale and another to collect the money. A customer who can't or won't pay you for goods or services delivered is worse than no customer at all! **If there's any question whether a new customer will pay you on a timely basis, refuse the business.**

A moving and storage company with a number of large commercial accounts never checked credit references. Because they required new customers to sign written contracts, they felt the company was fully protected and there was no need to check references.

The problem with this logic, of course, is that the best contract in the world isn't going to protect you if your customer can't pay his bills! The movers altered their practice and began securing credit references from all new accounts.

There are a number of tools available to help you verify the creditworthiness of a business. Dun and Bradstreet is one of the most widely used services, and can provide you with a credit report containing all the information you need to make a sound decision concerning new customers.

Another important way to protect yourself is to require all new business customers to fill out a detailed credit application before any credit is extended. Such an application should request specific references sufficient to allow you to verify that the new customer is in good standing.

Of course, you do have to follow through by checking the references that the customer provides, starting with the applicant's bank. Don't be bashful about asking your new customer to put you in touch with a specific individual at the bank who can discuss his creditworthiness.

Additionally, you can often get even more valuable information from the business references listed by your new customer. In contacting these commercial references, be sure to ask such pointed questions as:

•How difficult is the customer to do business with?

•How long has the reference had a business relationship with the credit applicant?

•Does the applicant dispute bills either occasionally or on a regular basis?

•Does the customer take advantage of purchase discounts, when available?

•Is the company a chronic complainer about delivery times, service, or the quality of products? (There are some business customers that absolutely no one can please. You certainly don't want to end up with that kind of problem in this economy.)

STRATEGY NUMBER 49: Check References Before Extending Credit to a New Customer

HOW DOES THIS APPLY TO MY BUSINESS? _____

_____

_____

_____

_____

Priority   1   2   3   *(circle one)*   Action date _____

Potential dollar effect $ _____

Person assigned to this strategy _____

50. Protect Your Company's Most Valuable Asset: Yourself

A severe economic recession doesn't just take a toll on a company's financial statement—it places enormous pressure on people, too.

I know many hard-working, experienced and normally successful business people who are undergoing tremendous personal strain as a result of current economic conditions.

Just the other day, one of my clients told me that his personal wealth had literally been wiped out as a result of his business problems. A year ago this individual had liquid assets of almost $1 million. As of last week, he was down to $200 in his bank account.

The wife of another client, a highly respected attorney in our area, told me that the strain of trying to keep his law practice together had affected this man's entire personality and was threatening their marriage. That same week I received similar calls from two other distraught wives who were considering divorce!

I've known people driven to the verge of suicide because of business reversals. Indeed, I once spent the night driving around with one client just talking him out of taking his life. I was afraid to leave him alone until I could get him into some professional counseling.

These are not just isolated examples. My brother, Louis, is a psychiatrist. He told me that he has never seen so many business executives coming in for psychiatric counseling. And when the economy started to nose downward, the number of anti-depressant drugs that he prescribed increased sharply.

Take a lesson from this. Don't let the strain of a business downturn put you out of commission. You're the most valuable player on your team and you have a responsibility to stay healthy—both physically and emotionally.

There are a number of stress-reducing techniques that psychiatrists recommend for harried business executives. One calls for the business owner to write the names of his most frustrating customers on raw eggs. What a relief it is to smash those eggs!

In the final analysis, your health is your responsibility. Resist the urge to work yourself into a sickbed. Get enough rest and exercise, keep yourself on a decent diet, and take time off to recharge your batteries.

During hard times, a vacation doesn't have to be a luxury cruise around the world or first-class tour of the capitals of Europe. A few days of R&R in the mountains, or at the beach might end up saving your sanity, your marriage, or even your business.

STRATEGY NUMBER 50: Protect Your Company's Most Valuable Asset: Yourself

HOW DOES THIS APPLY TO MY BUSINESS? _____

_____

_____

_____

_____

Priority   1   2   3   *(circle one)*   Action date _____

Potential dollar effect $ _____

Person assigned to this strategy _____

51. Ask Customers to Pay by Invoice Rather than by Statement

There are businesses today struggling under the weight of 12 percent to 15 percent interest rates, yet they routinely offer other companies interest-free use of their money for 60 to 90 days at a stretch! The fact that these other companies are customers is no justification for such questionable corporate generosity.

If you have regular customers whom you supply on a regular basis, send them an invoice with each shipment. Why wait 30 days for them to pay your bill? Actually, it's not really 30 days, if you think about it. If you ship goods on the first of the month, you send your bills out at the end of the month, and the terms require payment within 30 days of receipt, in effect you're offering your customers 59 days of interest-free use of your money.

If necessary, renegotiate payment terms with your customers or clients so that they understand that you expect payment when services are rendered or goods are received. If your customers balk, sit down with them and explain the situation to them.

In these days of constricted cash flow it is simply unacceptable for any business to have to wait 60 to 90 days for payment.

STRATEGY NUMBER 51: Ask Your Customers to Pay By Invoice Rather Than By Statement
HOW DOES THIS APPLY TO MY BUSINESS? _____
_____
_____
_____
_____

Priority   1   2   3   *(circle one)*   Action date _____
Potential dollar effect $ _____
Person assigned to this strategy _____

52. Start Sending Out Semi-Monthly Statements

The first casualty of a business downturn is cash flow. Even if you're fortunate enough to be in an industry where sales are holding up, when the economic climate turns chilly the payment practices of your customers may not be as reliable as they once were.

It's important, therefore, for you to explore ways to juice up your organization's cash flow. **One of the simplest ways to boost cash flow is to increase the frequency of your billings.**

There is nothing sacred about sending statements for products or services once each month for activity during that month. At least consider shifting to a twice a month or even weekly billing schedule.

Most businesses can send out statements on a more frequent basis. Certainly, doctors, lawyers and other professional people can adopt this approach, and many wholesalers and retailers are able do the same. If you send your bills out twice a month instead of once, you've obviously accelerated your organization's cash flow by at least two weeks. If you can do that on a regular basis, it may be enough by itself to solve your cash flow problems!

This approach also helps to reduce debt at the bank. Because you are securing the use of your money two weeks sooner, you are reducing the need to borrow and thereby trimming interest costs.

A law firm with monthly billings averaging $100,000, now sends out semi-monthly statements and they've increased their cash flow significantly.

For example, let's assume that our law firm started in business at the beginning of the calendar year, and that it was fortunate enough to collect all of its money in the month following the billing. By the end of its first year the firm would have billed its clients $1,200,000, but posted receipts totalling only $1,100,000. That's because payment for the services that it billed during the month of December would not be received until January of the next year.

Had the lawyers decided to bill twice a month instead of once, assuming the firm collected on the December 15 statement by December 31st, they would have received an additional $50,000 during the final month of the year. Instead of collecting only $1,100,000 during its first year in business, the firm's cash flow would have been $1,150,000. A cash flow increase of $50,000 would be welcome any time, but in a soft economy it could be a Godsend.

Another way to look at it is to recognize that by shifting to a semi-monthly billing system you can, in an otherwise bad year, painlessly boost cash flow by 1/24th. This means that 4.2 percent of your total cash collection could be accelerated by going to a semi-monthly billing system.

To be sure, there's a little additional clerical work involved, plus the extra postage to mail out statements twice monthly. But I bet if you work out a rough cost-benefit analysis of this strategy, you'll find that the advantages far outweigh the extra expense.

STRATEGY NUMBER 52: Start Sending Out Semi-Monthly Statements
HOW DOES THIS APPLY TO MY BUSINESS? _____

_____

_____

_____

_____

Priority   1   2   3   *(circle one)*   Action date _____

Potential dollar effect $ _____

Person assigned to this strategy _____

53. Use Stamped Self Addressed Envelopes to Speed Payments

When the survival of your business is at stake, you need every advantage available to you. Even a psychological advantage can be important.

For example, many businesses have found that if they **supply customers with a postage-paid, self-addressed envelope,** their invoice will get paid before others. Don't ask me why, but there's something psychological associated with the convenience of a pre-paid, self-addressed envelope accompanying a document.

I happened to be with a doctor who was paying his bills, and he told me that the first invoices he pays are the ones which include an accompanying envelope. There's less effort for him, and he appreciates the fact that the postage has been paid by his creditor.

Of course it may be difficult to cost-justify return postage if you are sending out thousands and thousands of invoices to one-shot purchasers who may never buy from you again. This may be particularly true if you're billing relatively small amounts on each invoice.

But if you send statements to the same group of regular clients or customers on a regular basis, including a stamped self-addressed envelope with your statement may certainly be worth a try.

Many companies have found it to be effective for getting paid a little faster than their competitors, and an inexpensive vehicle for creating good will.

A number of creative businesses have carried this technique a step farther in order to cement positive relationships with their customers. For instance, some companies place messages on the backs of their return envelopes such as: "Thanks for your business," "We look forward to serving you again," or "We appreciate your continued support."

Admittedly, I can't say for sure that such expressions of appreciation ever saved a single company from bankruptcy. And I certainly can't guarantee your business a dollar-and-cents pay-off if you print such a message on your return envelopes.

But I can tell you that no businessman ever lost a customer because he said "Thank You." And plenty lost customers because they didn't.

STRATEGY NUMBER 53: Use Stamped Self-Addressed Envelopes to Speed Payments

HOW DOES THIS APPLY TO MY BUSINESS? _____

_____

_____

_____

_____

Priority   1   2   3   *(circle one)*   Action date _____

Potential dollar effect $ _____

Person assigned to this strategy _____

54. Charge Interest on Delinquent Accounts

A good way to lose your best customers and replace them with marginal ones is pursue a listless collection policy. Indeed, **if you don't charge interest on delinquent accounts, you are penalizing your good customers and rewarding the deadbeats!**

Suppose, for example, you ship a $100,000 order to a great customer, and he pays you immediately. Then you fill a similar order for a different customer and "Company B" takes two months longer to pay. If you charge interest on overdue accounts at 18 percent annual percentage rate, the slow-paying customer will have to fork over an additional 1–1/2 percent for two months. That comes to an extra $3,000 in addition to the original $100,000 owed. In effect, "Company B" has paid $103,000, while prompt-paying "Company A" received the same merchandise from you for $100,000.

But if you don't charge interest, the opposite takes place. Your quality customer still pays $100,000, but you've effectively subsidized Mr. Slow Pay by giving him a discount of 1–1/2 percent a month for 60 days. In effect, Company B has really paid you only $97,000—and they inconvenienced you, to boot.

Even in the best of times, this is an effective way to attract "problem customers" that other companies don't even want to deal with. In bad times, you just can't afford this kind of marginal business.

An advertising agency with annual billings of almost $2,000,000, recently instituted a penalty for non-timely payment. During the first year under this new system the agency collected close to $25,000 in interest charges from late-paying accounts. For our client that $25,000 represented "found money" that could be used to reduce the company's debt. The agency wouldn't have had to borrow in the first place had all of its customers paid their bills in a timely fashion.

When you first begin charging interest on overdue accounts, it is important to communicate to your customers the new ground rules in advance. Send them a straightforward statement explaining that you will be charging an annual rate of 18 percent, or a 1–1/2 percent monthly delinquent charge for non-payment of bills.

In your letter explain your reasons for adopting the new policy, and offer late-paying customers two months to clean up their past due accounts. Make sure they know that if their accounts are not current at the end of this grace period, they will then incur interest charges.

(Of course, it's a good idea first to check the wording of your notice with your attorney to ensure compliance with all federal and state truth-in-lending laws.)

From a practical point of view, you have advised your customers that there is a penalty for not paying their bills on time. You've given them fair warning that there are consequences attached to inaction.

I've had clients tell me: "I can't charge my customers finance charges! They won't accept these penalties, they won't pay them, and they'll go to another company that doesn't charge them interests on late payments." In dealing with hundreds of businesses, I can tell you that I have never encountered a situation where a customer refused to do business with an organization because they imposed a finance charge. There's a basic sense of fairness in the marketplace and people realize that it's only reasonable for the parties responsible for these costs to incur the penalties.

Indeed, if a customer were to refuse to do business with you because of such a policy, that in itself would represent compelling evidence that the firm didn't intend to pay you on a timely basis in the first place.

Obviously, if a *good* customer does complain, it may be good business to write off that finance charge the first time. But be sure to let that company know that you won't do this on a continuing basis. If a customer believes that you will routinely excuse finance charges, it's likely he will continue to pay his bills late.

STRATEGY NUMBER 54: Charge Interest on Delinquent Accounts
HOW DOES THIS APPLY TO MY BUSINESS? _____

_____

_____

_____

_____

Priority   1   2   3   *(circle one)*   Action date _____
Potential dollar effect $ _____
Person assigned to this strategy _____

55. Resolve Customer Billing Disputes Promptly

Many businesses with serious collection problems are suffering from self-inflicted wounds. Every company has its share of slow-paying clients, bankrupt customers, and plain old bad apples who just won't settle their accounts without a fuss.

But some firms seem to be constantly embroiled in lengthy and counterproductive billing disputes with their customers. Check through your accounts receivable records for signs of such problems. **If more than 5 percent to 10 percent of your accounts are late because of fee disputes, you need to take corrective action.**

In dealing with our clients, we've found that there are three kinds of collection problems:

1. **The impossibles:** *customers who really can't pay you.* They are companies that are insolvent or bankrupt, or the owner has died. Don't waste a lot of time here. In these cases there's nothing you can do except get in line at the courthouse and try and recover something.

2. **The possibles:** *businesses which may be financially strapped, but are able to pay you.* They may not want to pay you, but if necessary they could go to a bank and borrow the money. When these clients say they can't pay you, what they're really saying is that they've made a decision to pay other people before you. These are the customers your accounts receivable people should be working on. A good credit manager can convince these businesses that it's important to pay your company before others.

3. **The possiblies:** *customers who are able to pay you but aren't paying because of a billing dispute.* You have to work on these accounts right away. Distinguishing this third group from the others and dealing effectively with these customers can be the key to a cash flow turnaround for many organizations.

Resolving customer billing disputes properly and promptly is doubly important because it offers you the chance to turn a problem into an opportunity and to cement a relationship with a potentially valuable customer.

The last time my wife returned merchandise to a department store, they neglected to credit our account. It was a simple billing error but it took four or five months to resolve. Meanwhile we kept receiving invoices for the incorrect amount and we had to write several letters to the company. By the time the account was finally straightened out, my wife was totally steamed and she vowed never to shop in that store again!

Now, suppose that same store had made a conscious effort to turn the situation around? Suppose they acknowledged the error promptly, then sent out a letter of apology asking you to contact a representative of the company if the problem is not corrected on the next monthly statement?

Imagine the amount of goodwill the department store would reap if all billing disputes were handled in this manner? Instead of being resentful toward the store, customers would have reason to believe that the company really appreciates their business. Isn't this the kind of organization you'd like to deal with? Instead of losing shoppers because of its billing practices, the store could be building long-term customer loyalty!

STRATEGY NUMBER 55: Resolve Customer Billing Disputes **Promptly**

HOW DOES THIS APPLY TO MY BUSINESS? _____

_____

_____

_____

_____

Priority   1   2   3   *(circle one)*   Action date _____

Potential dollar effect $ _____

Person assigned to this strategy _____

56. Shore Up Listless Collection Practices

It's been said that in a bad economy you have to work twice as hard to make half as much. Often the problem is not any lack of business, but rather an inability to get customers to pay for your goods or services.

If your business is hurting as a result of soft economic conditions, chances are your clients are having difficulties as well.

While we can and should sympathize with our hard-pressed customers, we must not allow their problems to drag us under. Poor collection practices are a prescription for disaster in the best of times. **During a business downturn it's even more important to establish effective collection procedures.**

Here's a game plan to put your company's collections back on track:

1. **Appoint a permanent manager to handle collections.** Too many businesses treat collections as a stepchild. When customers fall behind in payments, the company bookkeeper, or office manager or a secretary may be assigned to placing a "reminder" call. Often there's no real system, and clients are sometimes allowed to fall so far behind that they may never catch up.

If you have to go outside and hire someone to handle this, so be it. At an organization with cash flow problems, the money spent on a good collections manager will come back many fold.

2. **Put "problem" customers on C.O.D. or stop shipments altogether.** Many businesses continue to deliver service or ship goods when their clients fall far behind in their payments. It's important to let delinquent accounts know that you mean business.

3. **Secure personal guarantees from the owners of the business as well as from their spouses.** If a business goes down the tubes while owing you money, you're not going to be paid by the company. But if you've required the owners of the business to personally guarantee the debt, then the obligation is doubly secured. If the business fails, you have a legal right to recover personal as well as business assets. To be sure, business owners are often reluctant to secure business debt with personal assets—and well they should be (see Chapter 68). However, if you're the one extending credit to a financially troubled company, you should protect your business by insisting on personal guarantees.

4. **Always obtain a payment commitment from overdue accounts.** It's easy for a person to say, "I'll put a check in the mail." Set a deadline and if the customer doesn't meet it, contact the company immediately. Some businesses with effective collection procedures even send someone around to visit chronic slow-paying businesses on the day that each bill is

due. When you've agreed to make a payment on a specific date it's hard to wiggle out of your obligation if the bill collector is literally at the door.

5. Put your collections staff on commission. Collecting bills is tough work, especially in a soft economy. It's important to give your collections staff an incentive to go that extra mile on your behalf.

One building contractor pays his collections personnel a base salary plus a sliding scale commission to encourage aggressive collections. Under this system the staff is paid a bonus of 1 percent on collections of 60-to-90 day old accounts, 1–1/2 percent on collections of 90–120 day old accounts, and 2 percent on receipts from accounts older than 120 days.

The contractor also sets a quota to ensure that the collections staff actively seeks payments in less than 60 days. Those who don't make quota face a possible downward revision in their base salary. As a result of these collection incentives, the average age of the company's accounts receivables has dropped by almost two weeks! The upsurge in cash flow is just what the doctor ordered!

STRATEGY NUMBER 56: Shore Up Listless Collection Practices

HOW DOES THIS APPLY TO MY BUSINESS? _____

_____

_____

_____

Priority   1   2   3   *(circle one)*   Action date _____

Potential dollar effect $ _____

Person assigned to this strategy _____

57. Take Advantage of Purchase Discounts

In tough economic times, a 10 percent or 12 percent return on investment looks pretty good. A 24 percent return sounds fantastic! But suppose I told you many businesses can easily earn a whopping 36 percent on their money—and most of them let that opportunity slip through their fingers!

It's as simple as this: **schedule payments to suppliers to maximize purchase discounts.** In many industries it's customary for suppliers to discount for prompt payment. If you pay the bill 30 days in advance and the supplier rewards you with a 2 percent discount, then you're effectively earning a better return on your money than you can get from any bank! Figure it out for yourself. A 2 percent discount for allowing the supplier access to your money 30 days early doesn't mean you're receiving 2 percent a year. It means you're getting 2 percent a month! Multiply that by 12 months and you're earning interest on your money equal to 24 percent a year. That's not bad, but you can do better yet.

If the terms provide for a 2 percent discount on all bills paid by the tenth of the month, that doesn't mean you have to pay the bill 30 days early to take advantage of the savings. A payment 20 days early will qualify you for the discount, assuming your payment is due at the end of the month. If you earn 2 percent for paying a bill 20 days before it is due, then instead of a 24 percent return, your early payment has earned you an effective yield of 36 percent a year! (A return of 2 percent for 20 days is equivalent to 3 percent over a 30 day period. Multiply that 3 percent by 12 months and you're earning 36 percent a year!)

If you're cash-starved, go to a bank and borrow money in order to pay a bill 20 days early and receive the 2 percent discount. If the cost of borrowing at the bank is, say, 11 percent, and you earn 36 percent on your money, then you're still 25 percent ahead!

If your suppliers don't offer early payment terms, have a talk with them. In troubled economic times securing timely payments and holding on to customers who do pay promptly are prime considerations. There are plenty of businesses that can be coaxed into offering you a 2 percent discount for paying your bills by the tenth of the month. Indeed, most wholesalers or other distributors of goods or services would probably be more than willing to negotiate those kinds of terms, if they don't offer them already.

A medical practice has for years paid laboratory fees religiously on the 15th of the month. The owner prides himself on how his bills are always paid in such a timely fashion.

I suggested that the owner talk to the laboratory about a prompt payment discount. As it turned out, the lab was experiencing such severe collection problems that cash flow had become an overriding consideration. They readily agreed to offer him a 2 percent payment discount in return for his agreement to pay his bills on the tenth of the month rather than the 15th. Now he's enjoying a 36 percent return on his money.

STRATEGY NUMBER 57: Take Advantage of Purchase Discounts

HOW DOES THIS APPLY TO MY BUSINESS? _____

_____

_____

_____

Priority   1   2   3   *(circle one)*   Action date _____

Potential dollar effect $ _____

Person assigned to this strategy _____

58. Comparison Shop Supply Prices

When the economy sours and the success of your business is at stake, it's time to re-examine your standard operating procedures. Even little things, like making sure you are getting the best value for your business supply dollar, aren't really "little" when the company's future is on the line.

Many businesses purchase office supplies on the basis of convenience. At a convenience store you can park at the door, pick up a few items, and get out without standing around in long check-out lines. The downside, of course, is that you're paying a premium for this convenience.

Buying from an office supply distributor who sends a salesman directly to your facilities to take orders might well be cost-effective when business is brisk and your staff is working frantically to keep pace with the demand. But when sales are off and you're finding it difficult to keep your employees busy, you don't need to pay for convenience.

One of our clients had been buying office supplies from the same distributor for years. Our client thought it was a pretty good deal because in addition to getting "free" delivery, the supplier was giving him a 20% volume discount!

A big discount may be no bargain if your supplier's prices are uncompetitive to begin with. As it turned out, even with the supposed "20% discount" our client was paying $9.80 for a dozen yellow legal pads that could be purchased at a nearby discount office supply house for $5.90!

Other supplies purchased from the distributor were priced similarly. Instead of saving 20 percent, our client was paying 50 percent more than he needed to for his office supplies.

Make no mistake—I'm not saying that convenience and service have no value. When business is strong and time is short, it may well make sense to pay a premium for extra service. But when the reverse is true—when sales are sluggish and much of your organization is idle—you don't need to pay someone to save you time.

STRATEGY NUMBER 58: Comparison Shop Supply Prices

HOW DOES THIS APPLY TO MY BUSINESS? _____

_____

_____

_____

_____

Priority   1   2   3   *(circle one)*   Action date _____

Potential dollar effect $ _____

Person assigned to this strategy _____

SUPPLY COST COMPARISON

ITEM	QUANTITY	VENDOR	COST	DELIVERY

59. Secure Current Bids for All Major Expenditures

It's always good business policy to get up-to-date bids from several sources before making a significant financial commitment. When your company is experiencing hard times, securing competitive bids can be an even more important practice.

Take the case of the real estate investor who acquired a substantial parcel of land to develop as a shopping center. When the plans were originally drawn up two years ago, he obtained some very competitive bids to construct the necessary access roads and parking areas.

He was finally prepared to proceed with the project earlier this year. And he was very pleased that he had been able to nail down such attractive road construction bids two years earlier. Fortunately, however, before executing those bids he checked the market again in view of current business conditions.

Sure enough, with commercial construction in a tailspin, paving jobs were few and far between and the market far more competitive than it was two years ago. By getting a new bid, our client saved $1.5 million on that one contract!

In another example, an insurance company with ambitious expansion hopes had planned to build an office building to serve as its corporate headquarters. They secured competitive bids, lined up contractors, and were all set to break ground when the economy took a nosedive. Company executives quickly tabled the plan and decided to sit tight until the recovery.

Recalling the lesson learned by our friend the shopping center developer, we urged our insurance client to reconsider. They agreed to solicit new bids and, once again, the story had a happy ending.

As it turned out, the building contractors were willing to do the job at or near cost, just to cover overhead expenses and keep their crews working. The construction company landed a major project that helped it to survive the slump, and our client saved a cool $1 million on their new corporate office building.

The benefits of securing timely competitive bids aren't limited to construction projects. An international trading company has been buying its packaging materials and shipping crates from the same supplier for years. They decided to secure fresh bids to test current market conditions, and again the result was major savings. This year, instead of spending $300,000 for cardboard boxes, the shipper will spend $230,000.

Remember: **a sour economy often translates into a buyer's market, and there may be tremendous opportunities available to your company during these times.**

STRATEGY NUMBER 59: Secure Current Bids for All Major Expenditures

HOW DOES THIS APPLY TO MY BUSINESS? _____

_____

_____

_____

_____

Priority   1   2   3   *(circle one)*   Action date _____

Potential dollar effect $ _____

Person assigned to this strategy _____

60. Cash In On Interest-Bearing "Sweep" Checking Accounts

If you've never heard of a "sweep" account, you have plenty of company. Bankers don't promote these arrangements and many business owners who maintain large checking account balances are unaware of them. As a result, a lot of companies struggling to make ends meet are missing an opportunity for a real windfall.

"Sweeps" are essentially interest-bearing checking accounts for which you give the bank permission to invest, or "sweep," certain funds on a day-to-day basis. A typical arrangement could provide that any funds in the account in excess of, say, $25,000, may be invested in overnight paper.

You won't find these kinds of accounts listed among the services offered at your bank, and no banker worth his pinstripes is going to raise the possibility of a sweep with you. But if the bank does offer these arrangements and you ask about them, you should get the full story.

Take the case of the international mail order business that routinely keeps large amounts of cash on deposit for short periods. At any given time, this business averages at least $500,000 in its checking account.

When the vice president of the company's bank, with which it had been doing business for 30 years, was queried about the possibility of securing interest on its deposits, he replied: "A sweeps account? We've been offering those for the past ten years." The mail order house promptly filled out the paperwork and began earning interest the next day. For thirty years the bank had a free ride on their money—now it was our client's turn to pocket the increase.

A word of caution: "sweep" accounts are not FDIC-insured. If the bank fails, you may lose your money. Of course, even with a traditional account, FDIC only covers the first $100,000 on deposit. So if you have considerably more than that routinely sitting in a non-interest bearing checking account, you're not really risking anything by assigning the amount in excess of $100,000 to a "sweeps."

STRATEGY NUMBER 60: Cash In on Interest-Bearing "Sweep" Accounts

HOW DOES THIS APPLY TO MY BUSINESS? _____

_____

_____

_____

_____

Priority   1   2   3   *(circle one)*   Action date _____

Potential dollar effect $ _____

Person assigned to this strategy _____

61. Shift to Short-Term Leases to Limit Exposure

When profits are down and cash is short, prudent businesses often choose to lease rather than buy equipment, vehicles or facilities. If your company is at all vulnerable during a business downturn, however, **a long-term lease can be the shortest route to the poor house.**

When the economy is in a nosedive, the last thing you need is to be stuck with three more years of stiff lease payments on equipment or facilities that you're not even using. When the fiscal forecast is frosty, limit your exposure with short-term leases. This way, if the worst happens, you can simply return the equipment and you're off the hook.

To be sure, you will pay a higher rate if you lease on a short-term basis. Rent an Oldsmobile from Hertz and it might cost you $50 or $60 a day. Lease that same car for four years and you may get it for only $300 a month. But if you only need the car for a few days, it's silly to make a long-term commitment.

You would be surprised, however, at how many businesses become unnecessarily encumbered in long-range leasing agreements.

A construction business needed a lot of earth-moving equipment. When the economy soured, this company was really hit hard. The owner was lucky to be able to keep his crews working two weeks out of every month.

On a long-term basis, leasing a single piece of heavy equipment would have cost the company over $4,000 a month, even though it was idle for at least half that time. Worse yet, if business got even slower, the company was committed to making those payments rain or shine for two years.

As an alternative, the contractor sublet the equipment he needed from another sputtering construction firm on a short-term, week-to-week basis. The company wound up paying $2,000 a week—but only for the two weeks each month that the equipment was needed.

The end result was that the company was paying the same $4,000 a month as before, but now had the option of walking away from that arrangement if business conditions worsened, or if a better deal came along!

Of course, it's not always possible to reduce the duration of your lease commitment without increasing your net cost of leasing. But even if you end up paying more, it's often a prudent move to limit your exposure in bad times.

Say you have an opportunity to lease a photocopy machine for five years at $100 a month, or a total of $6,000. If, instead, you are able to negotiate a month-to-month lease for that same machine at $150 a month, it could be a much better deal.

If you take the long-term lease and the bottom falls out of your business, you'll be expected to continue making those payments even though there's nothing to photocopy and no revenues coming in to pay the lease.

If you hedge your bets by taking the short-term option, you can walk away from that arrangement as soon as conditions change. If the business collapses, the most you owe the leasing company is $150. If the economy recovers and the danger to your company passes, you may then decide to terminate that "expensive" short-term lease and shop for a "cheaper" long-term arrangement.

Point is: when there's danger in the air, keep your powder dry and your options open.

STRATEGY NUMBER 61: Shift to Short-Term Leases to Limit Exposure
HOW DOES THIS APPLY TO MY BUSINESS? _____
_____
_____
_____
_____

Priority   1   2   3   *(circle one)*   Action date _____
Potential dollar effect $ _____
Person assigned to this strategy _____

62. Renegotiate Lease Terms to Mesh With Business Cycles

All businesses feel the pinch to some degree during a soft economy. But seasonal businesses get a double dose of adversity. For many of these companies it's a real struggle just to keep the doors open during the off season. Add a sluggish economy and things can really become touch and go.

There are strategies that homebuilders, campground operators and other seasonal businesses can use to ease the pressure during slack periods. Since companies in seasonal industries are forewarned of the worst, they can be forearmed.

In the landscaping business, for example, you know that you will be generating virtually all of your revenues during spring, summer and fall. Nothing is going to be coming in during the winter, even in a booming economy. Wouldn't it be nice if your overhead costs dried up during the winter, too? Actually, that isn't so farfetched.

If you're a landscaper and you're leasing your equipment, it may be possible to **work out a schedule so that you make lease payments over a nine month period rather than 12 months.** It's hard enough making it through the winter without income—why saddle yourself with equipment payments in those months?

A real estate development firm leased millions of dollars worth of earth movers and other heavy equipment that couldn't be used in the winter months when the ground was frozen.

The company had been operating in this fashion for years, and likely still would be, had the bottom not fallen out of the construction market. Because of the downturn, the company failed to generate enough income during the "busy" season to continue the lease payments through the winter. They called an emergency meeting with the lessor and negotiated a new arrangement under which monthly payments would be due only from March through October.

The leasing company agreed to this change because it didn't affect the total amount paid on the equipment each year—the company was simply making fewer but larger payments. Additionally, by agreeing to the new schedule the leasing company assured the survival of one of its largest customers.

This isn't the only way for seasonal businesses to get relief from stiff, year-round lease payments. It may be possible to restructure a lease agreement from twelve to eight monthly payments without increasing the amount of each payment. Indeed, the lessor may jump at such a proposal if you, in turn, are willing to agree to an extension of the term of the lease.

STRATEGY NUMBER 62: Renegotiate Lease Terms to Mesh with Business Cycles

HOW DOES THIS APPLY TO MY BUSINESS? _____

_____

_____

_____

_____

Priority   1   2   3   *(circle one)*   Action date _____

Potential dollar effect $ _____

Person assigned to this strategy _____

63. Sell Off Idle Assets

Idle assets—unused vehicles, vacant real estate, or unneeded machinery—can derail a business's cash flow and grind an organization to a halt. Even assets that you own free and clear can create a painful profit drain.

For example, you may incur unnecessary but considerable maintenance and storage expenses, and continuing to hold on to an asset when it is no longer needed increases your casualty insurance costs. Adding insult to injury, in some states you may have to pay a personal property tax on that item.

In contrast, disposing of an idle asset can have an invigorating effect on your company's cash flow and your bottom line. If an unneeded asset is being financed and you can recover enough from the sale to allow repayment, disposing of a vacant factory or an unused truck will enable you to reduce your monthly note payment costs.

Even if an idle asset can't be sold, it may still be advantageous for you to get it off your books. You can donate it to a charitable organization and claim a tax deduction, subject, of course, to the limitations imposed by IRS rules.

If nothing else, most assets have some scrap or salvage value. Even trash may be worth something to somebody. Take the case of a medical practice which routinely purged its files of old, unneeded patient X-rays. The doctors were actually throwing away treasure with the trash. Because of the silver content in the film, this medical practice learned they could recycle the old X-rays at a tidy profit.

Perhaps the most compelling reason to reexamine the status of your business assets is the fact that you may be able to reap substantial tax benefits by unloading them. Indeed, your company may be able to claim a sizeable tax loss by disposing of idle assets—as long as they are sold for less than their "undepreciated basis" (the original acquisition cost less the depreciation claimed over the years).

For example, suppose that a dry cleaning business posted a net taxable income of $45,000 three years ago, but has since fallen on hard times. To raise cash, the owner decides to dispose of some cleaning equipment no longer needed because of a store closing. Let's say the equipment was purchased some years ago for $225,000. Over the years the company was able to tax-depreciate a total of $80,000 on that equipment. The remainder—$145,000—represents the undepreciated basis of the asset.

Now let's say the operator is able to sell the surplus equipment for $100,000. The remaining $45,000 represents a tax loss—an amount that can be used to reduce the company's federal income taxes. Since the business is currently operating in the red and has no tax liability, what good is that $45,000 tax loss? Plenty! Under the IRS code, a tax loss may be carried back three years and taxes paid in those previous years may be recovered.

In this example, our dry cleaner could carry back his loss, apply it retroactively to the taxes he paid three years earlier, and recover the $6,750 from IRS (15 percent tax rate X $45,000 = $6,750). Pennies from heaven!

STRATEGY NUMBER 63: Sell Off Idle Assets

HOW DOES THIS APPLY TO MY BUSINESS? _____

_____

_____

_____

_____

Priority   1   2   3   *(circle one)*   Action date _____

Potential dollar effect $ _____

Person assigned to this strategy _____

64. Keep Your Assets Liquid

In a weak economy, cash is king. Even billionaires can be humbled if they ignore this principle. Donald Trump had a very strong financial statement when he first began experiencing financial problems. Unfortunately for him, it was top-heavy on hotels, office buildings and other non-liquid assets.

You can't pay your bills with real estate or machinery—your creditors want cash. During tough times if you make any investments at all, be sure that they're not the kind that tie up your money for five to ten years. Instead, think in terms of a commitment of six months or less.

In general, **when business is bad, limit investments to highly liquid assets** such as certificates of deposit, mutual funds, savings accounts, treasury bills or notes, stocks, bonds or mutual funds.

During any downturn there are going to be investment opportunities that may appear very attractive to people with cash on hand. But if making that investment means exhausting or seriously reducing your liquidity in a soft economy, resist the temptation to go bargain-hunting.

A client of ours—an individual who amassed a considerable fortune as a retailer of consumer electronics—learned this the hard way. A year ago this particular business owner had a profitable and growing chain of stores, and a personal net worth of nearly $17 million, including $1 million in cash on hand. He was sitting on top of the world.

Much to the disapproval of his top advisors, he decided to invest heavily in Sunbelt real estate. Convinced that his investment would appreciate rapidly, he sunk all of his liquid assets into a single piece of commercial real estate in south Florida. At the same time he secured a $3 million bank loan to finance the purchase of a wholesale distribution company that was the principle supplier of his retail operation.

At this point our client's liquid assets were all gone, and so was his flexibility to respond to changing business conditions.

When the economy turned sour, our client's retail sales slowed considerably and profitability plunged. Complicating matters was the fact that an equipment loan was coming due requiring a sizeable balloon payment by the company. Unfortunately, our client couldn't turn to his newly-acquired wholesale operation to pick up the slack. Because the wholesale business was heavily dependent on the company's retail segment as a customer, it too began to struggle.

Suddenly, the owner had no income to pay off debts in the Florida venture, and he was dangerously close to defaulting on his balloon payment and on his $3 million note to the bank.

To stay afloat, our client needed about $400,000, pronto. Even though he still had total assets approaching $17 million, more than a dozen different banks turned him down cold!

Ultimately, he was able to secure a loan in time to make the balloon payment and save his business operations from foreclosure. But he lost his investment in the Florida property, and he had to use a significant amount of personal funds to help bail out his businesses.

As a rule of thumb, your business should have sufficient cash or other liquid assets to cover operating costs for three months. If you're unable to set aside this much capital, then at least arrange for a line of credit offering you access to this much cash, if it's needed in an emergency.

STRATEGY NUMBER 64: Keep Your Assets Liquid
HOW DOES THIS APPLY TO MY BUSINESS? _____

_____

_____

_____

_____

Priority   1   2   3   *(circle one)*   Action date _____
Potential dollar effect $ _____
Person assigned to this strategy _____

65. Use a Monthly Cash Flow Analysis to Forecast Financing Needs

The right time to secure financing is when your company is still healthy and your financial statements are strong; *the* worst time to borrow money for your company is when the business is in dire straits.

The trick is to determine your financing needs at least several months in advance. You can do this by developing a monthly cash flow analysis that will alert you to problems in advance.

Every business should be making monthly analyses projecting cash flow for the next 12 months. A number of computer software programs can help you prepare these types of projections for your company. With these analyses you can predict the lean months, anticipate cash flow crunches, and take corrective action well in advance.

Forewarned by the results of your monthly cash flow analyses, you can discuss your borrowing needs with your banker at a time when you still have a variety of options available to you. For their part, lenders are more than willing to work with businesses that display an ability to plan in advance and manage their own destiny.

Indeed, a banker would much rather deal with a business person who expresses a need for financing six months down the road in order to ride out the slow season, or replace aging equipment, or whatever. In contrast, businesses that wait until the last minute and then call the bank in a panic are risking rejection.

We have accompanied many of our clients to the bank armed with monthly cash flow analyses and invariably we get a warm reception. These projections eliminate the element of surprise for the banker, and that's half the battle in securing a loan.

STRATEGY NUMBER 65: Use a Monthly Cash Flow Analysis to Forecast Financing Needs

HOW DOES THIS APPLY TO MY BUSINESS? _____

_____

_____

_____

_____

Priority   1   2   3   *(circle one)*   Action date _____

Potential dollar effect $ _____

Person assigned to this strategy _____

66. Tap Your Life Insurance for Last Resort Financing

In the best of times, if you went to the bank for a loan you would expect to pay at least 11 percent or 12 percent for the money. Under less than ideal circumstances, you could count on being hit with somewhat higher interest rates. When your business is foundering and you're desperate for cash, you might be unable to secure bank financing at any price.

Many business owners, however, forget that they're sitting on a cheap and easily accessible source of financing—the cash value of the whole life insurance policies that they've taken out over the years, either personally or through the corporation.

If these policies have been in force for any period of time, you may have accumulated a considerable surrender value against which you are able to borrow.

Borrowing against the value of a whole life policy is a lot easier than trying to squeeze money out of a reluctant banker. Typically, you don't need collateral and it doesn't matter what shape your finances are in.

Moreover, you can tap into the accumulated value of such a policy at interest rates that would make a miser blush. If you've had your policy for twenty years or so, you may be able to borrow cash on it for as little as 4 percent. But even if your policy was taken out within the past five years, you might well be able to secure a loan on the policy at somewhere in the neighborhood of 8 percent. The icing, however, is that unlike a bank loan, money that you borrow on the cash value of your whole life insurance policy never has to be repaid!

As attractive as this financing alternative is, consider borrowing on a whole life insurance policy only when all else fails. This should be your last resort—the trump card you play when the chips are down. As long as you are able to line up other sources of financing, keep your life insurance as your ace in the hole.

Talk with your insurance agent about this, and at the same time ask for a rundown of all your current policies, premiums, and cash values.

STRATEGY NUMBER 66: Tap Your Life Insurance for Last Resort Financing

HOW DOES THIS APPLY TO MY BUSINESS? _____

_____

_____

_____

_____

Priority   1   2   3   *(circle one)*   Action date _____

Potential dollar effect $ _____

Person assigned to this strategy _____

67. Refinance Mortgages to Trim Interest Costs

Sometimes the opportunities that emerge during a bad economy can help to offset the hardships that we face in these times.

Case in point: interest rates typically decline during an economic downturn, and taking advantage of reduced credit costs by refinancing existing debt can be a critical survival strategy for your business.

As a rule of thumb, **if you own mortgaged property that you expect to keep for at least two years, consider refinancing when rates drop by 2 percent.**

We gave that advice to one of our clients who promptly checked with his bank and discovered that he could trim the interest rate on his home mortgage three percentage points. The loan origination fee and other closing costs worked out to only 2-1/2 points—an amount that he will be able to recoup in less than a year because of the three percent interest rate saving.

By refinancing, our client could reduce his monthly mortgage payments by over $200, and over the remaining years of the loan he would end up saving in excess of $24,000!

Since cash flow was not a problem for this particular individual, we suggested that instead of reducing his monthly payments by $200, he could refinance to reduce the term of his mortgage. Because of the lower interest rate, our client could pay off his mortgage in eight years instead of ten, while keeping the same monthly payments.

The bottom line is that he was able to eliminate 24 monthly payments on his home mortgage. At about $3,000 per month, our client saved $72,000!

In another example, a medical group practice purchased its own office building several years ago. They were able to obtain a $1 million mortgage on the building at 12 percent. When rates dropped below 10 percent, they explored refinancing options but found no takers. Because of the shaky economy, lenders had become extremely reluctant to finance commercial real estate.

One of the partners in the medical practice, however, owned a home in which he had $1 million in equity. The bank was more than happy to finance the doctor's residence. He used the $1 million that he borrowed on his home at 9 percent to pay off the 12 percent loan on the office building. The savings—3 percent of $1 million—equaled $30,000 a year.

The doctor did have a loan origination fee and other closing costs to pay. These fees came to roughly 2–1/2 points, or about $25,000. But the physician more than recouped these charges from his interest savings in the first year. Indeed, considering the 25-year term of the new mortgage, the effective annual cost of the refinancing was only $1,000 per year.

Points do become a very important consideration, however, for short term financing arrangements.

One enterprising entrepreneur buys houses at foreclosure, renovates them and then sells those residences at a tidy profit. From her standpoint, the best buying opportunities surface when the real estate market is weak. But this is exactly when it is most difficult to secure affordable financing for these projects.

She encountered a tremendous opportunity to purchase a number of properties, but the only financing she could arrange was through a private investor who wanted 19 percent interest plus five points!

The first house that she purchased under this arrangement required a total of four months to rehabilitate and resell. On an annualized basis, the price she paid to finance this transaction was enormous. An interest rate of 19 percent is bad enough, but to pay five points for a four-month loan computes out on an annualized basis to an additional 15 percent! Altogether, she was paying an effective annual rate of 34 percent!

This particular individual owned her personal residence free and clear, and it had been appraised at $500,000. Her bank, which would not finance her building renovation projects, was willing to provide her with an 80% mortgage on her home at 9 percent plus 2 points.

She jumped at the deal, stopped borrowing 34 percent money and used her 9 percent money instead. The savings were gigantic. On an annual basis, for every $100,000 that was borrowed to finance the purchase and renovation of foreclosure properties, she was able to save $25,000!

STRATEGY NUMBER 67: Refinance Mortgages to Trim Interest Costs

HOW DOES THIS APPLY TO MY BUSINESS? _____

_____

_____

_____

_____

Priority   1   2   3   *(circle one)*   Action date _____

Potential dollar effect $ _____

Person assigned to this strategy _____

68. Shield Your Personal Assets From Creditors

If you learn nothing else from this book, remember this: **don't use personal assets to secure company debts, and** *never* **allow your spouse to sign for a business loan.**

When you go to a bank for a loan, the banker will try to get as much collateral as possible from you. As a result, many loans are over-collateralized and the businesses that agree to these terms are suffering because of them.

One entrepreneur is in dire straits today because of this very problem. He purchased a piece of raw land in an area that had been growing rapidly when the economy was booming. The lender was all too willing to provide financing—as long as the investor and his wife agreed to personally guarantee the loan. Unfortunately, the investor accepted those terms.

Now, because of the slowdown in the economy, the unfortunate entrepreneur can't sell the property, and he certainly can't undertake the risk of developing it. Although he has been able to manage the monthly payments on the note, there is a $2.5 million balloon payment coming up, and it may just burst his bubble.

Because the value of the land has dropped, if the lender forecloses on the property the proceeds from the sale may not be enough to satisfy the loan. In that case, the bank will be able to seize the investor's personal property to satisfy the debt.

Worse yet, because the investor's wife also signed the note, the bank can also go after her property as well as all assets held jointly by the couple, including their home.

The advice I give to our clients is to offer lenders as little collateral as they have to, and treat their family assets as an ace in the hole. The wise ones follow that advice.

One business owner recently applied for a loan of approximately $1 million to modernize her operations. The bank agreed, but asked for a second trust on all of the company's real estate. In addition, the lender demanded that all of the business's other assets be put up as security, and that both the owner and her spouse personally guarantee the note.

If she had agreed to these demands and needed to borrow additional funds at a future date, she would have been out of luck . . . and possibly out of business. All of her assets—business as well as personal—would have been tied up to secure that note. There would have been no collateral available to obtain additional financing.

With our encouragement, the business owner balked at the bank's demands, and the lender ultimately agreed to take only $1.2 million of collateral on the $1 million loan.

In another example, a law firm with cash flow problems recently applied for a business loan, only to be told by the bank that it would be necessary for the spouses of the partners to personally guarantee the firm's indebtedness. Following our advice, the lawyers told the lender that this was unacceptable, and that they would not do business with the bank under such conditions.

Ultimately, they struck a compromise. Instead of requiring the partners' wives to co-sign the loan, the bank agreed to a plan under which life insurance policies of the partners were assigned to the bank as collateral.

If the law firm fails because of the death of one of the partners, the bank is protected from loan default by the proceeds of that partner's life insurance policy. But even if the worst happens, the jointly-held personal wealth of the partners and their families will not be in jeopardy. This way, if the law firm becomes unable to pay the loan and the lender is forced to foreclose, all the assets of the business could be lost. But even if the worst happens, the personal wealth of the partners and their families will not be in jeopardy.

STRATEGY NUMBER 68: Shield Your Personal Assets From Creditors

HOW DOES THIS APPLY TO MY BUSINESS? _____

_____

_____

_____

_____

Priority   1   2   3   *(circle one)*   Action date _____

Potential dollar effect $ _____

Person assigned to this strategy _____

69. Make Daily Deposits to Boost Cash Flow

It's incredible how many businesses hold payment checks and cash receipts for days on end before getting that money to the bank.

All businesses should make daily deposits. **There's absolutely no excuse for letting badly-needed cash sit idle in a drawer** when it can be used to reduce the need for borrowing.

Even if you're uncertain how to record a particular payment, don't just sit on the check. As a general rule, deposit your receipts first and worry about the bookkeeping later.

An automobile body shop had been experiencing chronic cash flow difficulties, but surprisingly the company cashier's drawer contained literally thousands of dollars in checks from insurance companies for work done by the body shop. The cashier had never taken them to the bank because he was unable to match customers with the insurance payments. Some of the checks gathering dust in the drawer were more than six months old, yet the bookkeeper was still awaiting clarification from the insurer.

Obviously, those checks could have been photocopied for later investigation and then immediately deposited in the company's account. By not following this procedure the company's cash flow problems were unnecessarily aggravated, and operating costs were needlessly increased.

The company might well have avoided some interest costs on business indebtedness had this money been put to use in a timely fashion.

Additionally, at many banks interest rates on loans are linked to the balance that the business maintains at that institution. The more quickly your receipts are deposited at the bank, the higher your firm's average account balance will be.

Another reason for making daily deposits is to reduce the risk of loss. I've seen situations where bookkeepers allowed cash receipts to pile up for several days because it was inconvenient to make daily deposits. In the event of a theft, however, the insurance company may well refuse to cover the loss on grounds that maintaining this much cash on hand exceeds the limits of the policy.

Moreover, if you allow checks to gather dust for months as our auto body client did, you may discover too late that they are worthless.

When a check is six months old, the bank is no longer obliged to accept it. Of course, you would be able to get the check reissued, but that's not at all certain. In a sour economy, the customer who paid you by check six months ago might not be in business today.

STRATEGY NUMBER 69: Make Daily Deposits to Boost Cash Flow

HOW DOES THIS APPLY TO MY BUSINESS? _____

_____

_____

_____

_____

Priority   1   2   3   *(circle one)*   Action date _____

Potential dollar effect $ _____

Person assigned to this strategy _____

70. Use Spare Cash To Pay Down Lines of Credit

Without the money to modernize facilities, hire additional employees, and expand into new markets, a company may miss out on opportunities that can ensure the success of the enterprise.

In bad times, however, the debt that a business accumulates can eat away at your organization from within. Indeed, this has been the ruin of thousands of companies, from mom and pop operations to giant multinational corporations.

If your business is fortunate enough to have some extra cash available, one of the smartest moves you could make might be to reduce the company's debt. At the same time, however, one of the dumbest moves you could make might be to repay debt.

The reason for this apparent contradiction is that not all debt is the same. Let's say your company has the good fortune to have $1 million on hand, and that you've got those funds in Certificates of Deposit earning you 7-1/2 percent. Suppose at the same time that your firm enjoys an open line of credit from a lender, and that you have borrowed several million dollars on that line at 11-1/2 percent interest.

If you were to liquidate your CDs at the first opportunity and use the proceeds to reduce the unpaid balance on your credit line, your company would be money ahead. The difference between the interest you're receiving on your CDs and the rate you're paying on the line of credit is 4 percent. On $1 million, that translates into $40,000 a year on the bottom line!

Suppose, however, that one of your competitors was in the same boat as you—$1 million in 7-1/2 percent CDs and a loan for which the firm is paying 11-1/2 percent. In the case of "Company X," however, let's say that instead of a line of credit obligation, your competitor owes money on some machinery.

If Mr. X liquidates his CDs and reduces his equipment loan debt, his company will also save $40,000 each year. But unlike you, your competitor may have made a fatal mistake.

A line of credit is a renewable resource. If you pay it down and discover later that your business needs funds, you can easily re-borrow.

Other debt, such as your competitor's equipment loan, is typically not renewable. Paying off this type of loan in a bad economy can be risky business. If you do pay off such a debt and subsequently discover that you need to re-borrow funds, you may not be able to do so.

STRATEGY NUMBER 70: Use Spare Cash to Pay Down Lines of Credit

HOW DOES THIS APPLY TO MY BUSINESS? _____

_____

_____

_____

_____

Priority   1   2   3   _(circle one)_   Action date _____

Potential dollar effect $ _____

Person assigned to this strategy _____

71. Pay Bills When They're Due—But Not Before

It's amazing how many business people pride themselves on paying their bills the moment they come in. Invariably, these people justify this practice as a means of enhancing their credit standing.

Their logic is faulty. **You don't wind up with any better credit by paying bills early, rather than when they're due.** Especially in tough times, creditors are very pleased to get their money when it is due. They certainly don't expect to be paid any sooner.

If your company is incurring finance costs by borrowing working capital from a bank, it makes absolutely no sense to provide your creditors with interest free use of your funds.

The people responsible for accounts payable at your company should be instructed to sort through all bills as they are received, and categorize them according to when they must be paid. Most bills are due either at the end of the month, by the 10th of the month, or by invoice. If the bill does not indicate when payment is due, it becomes your call to decide when it should be paid. It's a good idea to set up a "tickler file" to ensure that bills are paid at the appropriate time.

If you're really compulsive about paying bills before they are due, then at least contact your suppliers and negotiate a special early payment discount.

Although the general rule is to pay bills when they are due, there are times when it is wise to delay payments beyond the due date.

If you rent space for your business, your lease almost certainly obligates the landlord to provide certain services—heating, electricity, cleaning, maintenance, etc. If the landlord does not provide these services, you may well be justified in withholding payment until the services are restored.

For instance, a real estate brokerage had a very difficult time getting its landlord to maintain building temperature to the specifications of the tenants. In addition, the roof leaked, and the grounds were not being maintained.

After failing to convince the landlord to fulfill his obligations, the realtor began withholding rent payments. Over the course of six months, he withheld rent payments totalling some $350,000. Of course, this money was ultimately paid to the landlord. But in the interim the realtor was able to deposit this money in an interest-bearing savings account for a number of months, and reap a tidy return. Best of all, the landlord learned a lesson, and building maintenance was never again a problem for our client.

Likewise, businesses should consider delaying payments for orders which have not been delivered, or in cases where the supplier ships the wrong products or materials.

STRATEGY NUMBER 71: Pay Bills When They're Due—But Not Before

HOW DOES THIS APPLY TO MY BUSINESS? _____

_____

_____

_____

Priority   1   2   3   *(circle one)*   Action date _____

Potential dollar effect $ _____

Person assigned to this strategy _____

72. Exercise Dormant Lines of Credit

To a businessman, a line of credit is like a parachute. Hopefully, you'll never have to use it, but in a pinch it can be a real lifesaver.

The time to arrange for a line of credit is well before you feel that pinch. Many people secure credit lines when business is good, then forget about them until the crunch hits. That can be a prescription for disaster, however.

Trouble is, in a slow economy, bankers are quick to pull in their horns. During a downturn, **if your line of credit has been inactive for some time, the bank may terminate your account with little or no warning.**

A prominent and very successful physician had a line of credit of $100,000. He secured that line years ago, but never used it. It was an umbrella stored in the closet for a rainy day.

When the economy nosedived, the doctor's collections fell off and his cash flow dried to a trickle. No problem, though. He just wrote himself a check for $20,000 from the credit line, deposited it in his checking account, and used that money to pay all his business and personal bills. Suddenly, however, all of those checks started bouncing!

As it turned out, the credit line check was no good. Because there had been no activity on the account for several years, the lender terminated the credit line. Supposedly, a notice had been sent to the physician at that time, but he didn't recall seeing it. The damage was done in any event.

This situation could have cascaded into a real catastrophe for the doctor. With the help of a good credit rating and some fancy footwork, however, the physician was able to secure $20,000 from other sources, and all the checks that he wrote were ultimately honored. But it certainly was a very embarrassing episode.

You can avoid similar problems by giving your line of credit a little periodic exercise. Lenders aren't likely to terminate an account that is active and in good standing. Even if you don't need funds, it may be wise to borrow on your credit line occasionally.

Let's say you're able to secure a line of credit of $100,000, and you want to make sure it will remain active and available to you in a crunch. Every year or two, you could write yourself a loan for $100,000, place those funds in an interest-bearing account for a month, then pay back the line.

Suppose the spread between the interest charged by the lender and the rate you receive on your deposits is 3 percent. The cost to you of exercising your credit line would then be $250 ($100,000 X 3 percent X 1/12). That's a dirt cheap way of ensuring continued access to a $100,000 parachute!

STRATEGY NUMBER 72: Exercise Dormant Lines of Credit

HOW DOES THIS APPLY TO MY BUSINESS? _____

_____

_____

_____

_____

Priority   1   2   3   *(circle one)*   Action date _____

Potential dollar effect $ _____

Person assigned to this strategy _____

73. Use a Bank "Lock Box" to Maximize Interest on Deposits

Time is money, and when your business is struggling for its survival, you can't afford to waste either one. When funds are in the bank, even overnight, someone is being paid for the use of that money. When it's your money, that someone might as well be you.

If your business receives substantial income through the mail, you can **boost earnings on deposits with a 'lock box' from the bank.** Under these arrangements, when your customers put a payment in the mail to you, the check goes directly to the bank. The bank then records these receipts for you and deposits the checks into your account on the spot.

Some bankers charge a fee for lock box accounts but others make them available as a free service to their customers.

If you market goods or services through the mail, or by phone, or via direct-to-consumer advertisements, you should consider such an arrangement. Even if your company doesn't receive many checks through the mail, if those payments are large enough, a lock box account may be a great investment.

For example, a marketer of scientific equipment didn't receive many checks in the mail, but those that did come in were usually for amounts in excess of $100,000 each. Standard operating procedure at this company was to post all of the checks received during the previous day, and then deposit them in the bank on the third day.

Because of the large sums involved, the company decided to have these payments sent directly to a lock box at the bank. Now those funds are deposited immediately through the lock box, and the bank has standing orders to use that money to reduce the company's debt.

In this particular case, by using a lock box the company's interest costs will be shaved by at least $20,000 a year!

In addition to these direct savings, lock boxes also reduce the risk of loss through theft or embezzlement, and they can eliminate some bookkeeping chores for your company.

Banks typically provide you with regular computerized reports on the activity of your lock box, and some even make it possible for you to monitor your account by using your own computer and modem to tap into their records.

A word of caution, however. If you arrange for a lock box account, be sure to instruct the bank to contact your office prior to depositing any check that's marked "Payment in Full." If you deposit such a check and it turns out to be just a partial payment or only the first of several installments, you may have difficulty collecting the balance.

STRATEGY NUMBER 73: Use a Bank "Lock Box" to Maximize Interest on Deposits

HOW DOES THIS APPLY TO MY BUSINESS? _____

_____

_____

_____

_____

Priority   1   2   3   *(circle one)*   Action date _____

Potential dollar effect $ _____

Person assigned to this strategy _____

Part IV

Personnel Resources

74. Put a Freeze on Hiring and Routine Raises

It truly is an ill wind that blows no good at all, and there are valuable lessons for businesses to learn during difficult times. One of the most important of these is to work lean and mean.

A bloated organization is at a serious disadvantage under the best of conditions. When you're struggling to keep your company afloat, excess baggage can drag the whole ship under.

Overstaffing is a lot more common than you may think. Many businesses get used to keeping surplus employees on the payroll in good times, almost as a kind of security blanket for the management. You really don't need all those people, but it feels good to know that they're around just in case.

When business turns sour, however, and you're straining to make payroll, surplus employees are an anchor around your neck. Don't wait for things to get that bad. At the first whiff of trouble, **slap a moratorium on hiring and reduce staff through attrition.**

Not long ago, a small apparel retailer in our town had 47 people on the payroll. If you had asked the personnel director, he would have argued you into the ground justifying the need for every one of those people.

When the economy started to slide, the store began feeling the pinch right away. The owner didn't lay off anyone, but he did put a freeze on all new hiring. As people quit their jobs, they were not replaced and normal employee turnover did the job for him.

Since then, seven people have left the store, the staff is down to 40, and all the work is still getting done. The employees who are still with the company understand the economic situation and appreciate the fact that they still have jobs. As a result, they are willing to pitch in, work a little harder and pick up the slack.

For his part, the store owner avoided painful lay-offs yet still managed to reduce his payroll costs by almost $100,000. More importantly, though, the retailer learned a lesson that will continue paying dividends when the economy turns around.

For this particular businessman, the recession may actually prove to be a blessing in disguise. When it's over, his organization will be lean, trim and ready to make waves in the marketplace.

STRATEGY NUMBER 74: Put a Freeze on Hiring and Routine Raises
HOW DOES THIS APPLY TO MY BUSINESS? _____

_____

_____

_____

_____

Priority   1   2   3   *(circle one)*   Action date _____

Potential dollar effect $ _____

Person assigned to this strategy _____

75. Use Independent Contractors to Slash Payroll

Anyone who has ever had to make a payroll knows that the wages paid to regular "W-2" employees are just part of a business's total labor costs. Payroll taxes plus the cost of health insurance, paid holidays and vacations, and other "fringe benefits" average out to an additional 20 percent to 30 percent at most companies.

During hard times, high payroll costs can be a real killer. But **you may be able to ease the pinch significantly by relying on independent contractors.**

In contrast to a regular, salaried employee, there are no fringe benefit costs or payroll taxes to pay an independent contractor. Even if you have to lay out 10 percent or 20 percent more to secure the services of an independent contractor, you may be dollars ahead in the final analysis.

Aside from the obvious payroll savings, there may be other advantages to using independent contractors.

A wholesaler of lawn and garden supplies owned an extensive fleet of delivery trucks and employed a number of drivers for those vehicles. Unfortunately, the business had a terrible time attracting employees with decent driving records. The company's drivers were constantly being cited for traffic violations, and there were accidents almost every week.

As a result, our client's motor vehicle insurance rates went through the roof! Literally all of the distributor's profit was being soaked up by sky-high insurance premiums! If this had continued, the wholesaler would have been out of business in six months.

Fortunately, the owner recognized the problem and replaced his accident-prone drivers by contracting with an outside delivery service. Our client was able to get a terrific deal on this because the delivery service did not have to supply vehicles —just drivers to operate the company's existing truck fleet.

Best of all, the wholesaler was able to eliminate his insurance premiums altogether, because his fleet was covered by the delivery service's policy.

Since the contract drivers had first-rate driving records, the wholesaler's insurance costs dropped back to earth. In the end, the shift to independent contractors saved this company over $300,000 a year, and turned red ink into black.

STRATEGY NUMBER 75: Use Independent Contractors to Slash Payroll

HOW DOES THIS APPLY TO MY BUSINESS? _____

_____

_____

_____

_____

Priority   1   2   3   *(circle one)*   Action date _____

Potential dollar effect $ _____

Person assigned to this strategy _____

76. Shave Labor Costs with Part-Timers

When a business is fighting for its survival, it needs the best people it can get. But these days, many of the excellent workers simply aren't available for full-time employment.

A mother with small children may be unwilling to return to the workforce full-time, but she may be very interested in a job for few hours each day.

A retiree may not be interested in rejoining the rat race five days a week, but may well accept employment for a couple of days a week.

A college or professional school student may be unable to work regular hours, but might be a perfect candidate for evening or weekend employment.

Nowadays, employers are able to choose from an army of part-time job candidates who can make motivated and dedicated workers. Many have strong job experience, top skills and a great work ethic. It would be a shame to close off consideration of such people just because they're unable to work 40 hours a week, Monday-through-Friday.

But there's another good reason to consider employing part-time employees. **Part-timers can help you hold down labor costs!** Indeed, you may well discover that some of the positions you were filling with full-time workers don't really require 40 hours a week!

If a job can be done in 30 hours a week instead of 40, the employer may be able to reduce the cost of labor for that function by 25 percent a year. Save 10 hours each week at $10 an hour, and by the end of the year you're ahead $5,200!

Moreover, in many states if an employee works less than 17–1/2 hours a week, it's not necessary to provide that person with fringe benefits, even if you offer them to full-timers.

A manufacturer in our area was really feeling the squeeze as a result of the rising cost of employee benefits. The company was spending an average of $6,000 a year per worker just for "fringes." The manufacturer responded by converting 20 full-time positions into 40 part-time jobs.

All the stations are being manned, just as before, and the company is paying just as much in wages as it was previously. But because the company doesn't provide fringe benefits to part-timers, the manufacturer is money ahead. Indeed, eliminating $6,000 in fringe benefits to 20 employees is the same as adding $120,000 annually to the bottom line.

STRATEGY NUMBER 76: Shave Labor Costs With Part-Timers

HOW DOES THIS APPLY TO MY BUSINESS? _____

_____

_____

_____

_____

Priority   1   2   3   *(circle one)*   Action date _____

Potential dollar effect $ _____

Person assigned to this strategy _____

77. Reshuffle Staff Duties to Control Costs

Written job descriptions are valuable tools for any organization. But they aren't carved in marble. If you're finding it difficult to generate enough business to keep your staff busy, it's time to **broaden the work responsibilities of your employees.**

The management of an employment agency saved nearly $12,000 by rethinking the duties of just one employee. Billings were down sharply. The office manager was told to trim some fat from the firm's budget. That same day she discovered an employee camped out in the office conference room poring over the latest pulp novel. Business had become so slow, he explained, that he always had lots of spare time in the afternoons.

Most managers would have reacted by simply reprimanding the employee. To her credit, though, the office manager gave the situation a good bit of thought and decided to put this worker's "spare time" to work for the agency.

His new job duties, she decided, would include delivering payroll packages to each of the agency's five branch offices. Previously, the firm had used an outside messenger service to make those deliveries. By assigning these responsibilities to an otherwise idle employee, the office manager saved our client $12,000 a year in delivery charges.

Admittedly, not every organization needs regular messenger service. But practically every business can come up with ideas to make better use of idle employees.

When cash is tight, for example, couldn't some of your company's maintenance work be done by your own employees? And why not assign existing staff people to paint offices, landscape grounds, maintain company equipment, shop for office supplies or make minor building repairs?

Some employees may balk at such suggestions, but others will welcome new assignments as a break from the ordinary work routine. In any event, when the business is in trouble and the boss is battling to keep the company afloat, there's no reason why all employees shouldn't pitch in and assume some additional duties.

Make a list of services that you're currently paying outsiders to provide, then list the names of your employees who have the skills or experience to handle those chores in house. You may be in for a surprise!

STRATEGY NUMBER 77: Eliminate Employee Overtime
HOW DOES THIS APPLY TO MY BUSINESS? _____

_____
_____
_____
_____

Priority   1   2   3   *(circle one)*   Action date _____
Potential dollar effect $ _____
Person assigned to this strategy _____

78. Eliminate Employee Overtime

If business is slack but you're still paying overtime, something is wrong. Too often the problem is that overtime work has become the rule rather than the exception. In effect, these companies are operating on "permanent overtime!" After a while, some employees tend to regard overtime pay as a "fringe benefit" to which they are entitled, whether the company needs extra work or not. Indeed, some workers come to depend on that extra income and they become very creative at finding ways to make sure it continues.

Although state overtime ground rules vary, the national standard is clear: unless your employees are exempt from the Federal Fair Labor Standards Act because they hold managerial, professional or administrative status, you must pay them premium "time-and-a-half" pay for any hours worked in excess of 40 per week.

At 150 percent of an employee's normal hourly wage, overtime pay scales are difficult to swallow in the best of times. During a slump, premium wage rates can put you in the poorhouse. Before that happens, **impose a company-wide moratorium on overtime pay.** At a minimum, require written authorization from a key management official before any non-exempt employee works more than 40 hours per week.

Such a policy can eliminate a lot of misunderstandings as well as a lot of unnecessary payroll costs. A medical practice learned this the hard way. For years the doctors employed an office assistant who routinely worked 50 hours a week. Her regular salary came to around $20 per hour, but at time-and-a-half for those additional ten hours, this practice was paying her $300 dollars extra every week. When you add it all up, that comes to a $15,000 annual bonus on top of her regular salary!

Her "permanent overtime" was especially puzzling during a recent business downturn, since the workload had dropped drastically. When the doctors finally put an end to all employee overtime, there was no noticeable decline in productivity. But there was a whopping $15,000 bottom line savings to the practice.

The point to remember is that the opportunity to work overtime should not be something your staff takes for granted. If employees don't get the job done in 40 hours, then they should be prepared to explain why.

OVERTIME APPROVAL

Employee Name: _____

Department: _____

Project: _____

Estimated Overtime Hours: _____

Reason Overtime is Required: _____

_____

_____
Signature/Department Supervisor

_____
Date

STRATEGY NUMBER 78: Eliminate Employee Overtime

HOW DOES THIS APPLY TO MY BUSINESS? _____

_____

_____

_____

_____

Priority   1   2   3   *(circle one)*   Action date _____

Potential dollar effect $ _____

Person assigned to this strategy _____

79. Shift to a Six Hour Workday

It can take an organization years to recruit and develop a first-rate staff. But during tough times there simply may not be enough business coming in to justify your pre-recession payroll.

This situation creates a real "Catch 22" for business managers. On one hand, the company may not survive the recession unless labor costs are reduced. But if the firm lets valuable people go, it may find itself crippled when the turnaround comes.

The staff that the company will hire after the recession may not be half as good as the group that was laid off.

Some organizations faced with this dilemma have found a way to straddle the fence and reduce payroll costs without losing key personnel. Under their strategy, instead of laying off, say, 25 percent of your employees, you would **switch from an eight hour workday to six hours and cut salaries by 25 percent.**

Asking people to swallow a 25 percent pay cut may sound like a hard sell, but you just might be surprised. If your employees are aware of the difficult business conditions and are informed of the alternative, they're likely to be very supportive. At least this way everyone will still have a job, and when the economy turns around, the company can switch back to a full-time workshift.

As an alternative to a reduced workday, it may be possible to shift to a four day workweek—a 20 percent reduction.

Either way you will be saving jobs and providing your employees with more time to spend with their families, take courses, or just unwind.

Still another approach is to offer your staff the option of switching to part-time status. Many employees prefer working fewer hours, but simply have never had the nerve to ask.

A computer software design firm, for instance, made such a proposal to its staff in response to declining sales, and it worked like a charm. As an alternative to reducing the staff by 20 percent, the owner offered each worker the option of working fewer hours. As it turned out, almost a third of the staff wanted to be part-timers, and they jumped at the offer.

As a result, the part-time "wanna-bees" were happy, the "busy bees" who wanted to continue working full-time were able to do so, and nobody lost their job.

Everybody won, including our client.

STRATEGY NUMBER 79: Shift to a Six Hour Workday

HOW DOES THIS APPLY TO MY BUSINESS? _____
_____
_____
_____
_____

Priority   1   2   3   *(circle one)*   Action date _____

Potential dollar effect $ _____

Person assigned to this strategy _____

80. Hire In-House Mechanics to Service Vehicles and Equipment

If you can't make good on a promised delivery or service call because one of your vehicles is in the shop, you're likely to have a very disappointed customer. And when business is tight, you can't afford to disappoint anybody.

You can't always count on outside mechanics to adjust to your schedules and those of your customers. Just try to find a shop to service your company vehicles on a Sunday, or after hours on a week day.

Some companies incur the often considerable expense of leasing and maintaining extra vehicles just as back-ups for when their fleet is in the shop.

Other businesses, however, have found that they can **cut the cost of maintaining company vehicles and equipment by using in-house mechanics.**

During a business downturn there are plenty of unemployed mechanics who would be more than happy to work evenings and weekends to keep your fleet on the road during the work week.

A key advantage to handling vehicle and equipment maintenance internally is that it affords you the opportunity to practice "preventive medicine"—not just "emergency room treatment." Any health insurance company will tell you it's far cheaper to keep patients healthy than to pay for their hospital bills once they get sick.

It certainly worked out that way for one building contractor who hired his own mechanics to service the 60 vehicles in the company's fleet. By handling these chores internally, the contractor was able to reduce maintenance costs by some $50,000 a year. As an added bonus, because the vehicles were assured of receiving regular scheduled servicing by the company's mechanics, the trucks experienced fewer breakdowns and lasted longer.

A landscaping company had similar success when they brought in their own mechanics. This business owned and maintained literally hundreds of lawnmowers—dozens more than they needed. The owner's philosophy was "better safe than sorry," and he acquired all this extra equipment in case the regular mowers needed repairs or servicing.

By hiring a mechanic to perform needed repairs and maintenance during the evening hours, this landscaper not only reduced the cost of servicing these machines, but also eliminated the need for maintaining surplus equipment. During the first year alone, this lowered the company's costs by nearly $35,000.

STRATEGY NUMBER 80: Hire In-House Mechanics to Service Vehicles and Equipment

HOW DOES THIS APPLY TO MY BUSINESS? _____

_____

_____

_____

Priority   1   2   3   *(circle one)*   Action date _____

Potential dollar effect $ _____

Person assigned to this strategy _____

81. Brain-Pick Your Key Management Team

Your staff may know more about the day-to-day problems that chip away at the business's profitability than you do. They're also likely to be a wealth of information and advice on correcting those problems.

In hard times, it's a crying shame to ignore any potential source of help—especially the "experts" within your own organization. But **don't wait for them to speak up—ask your key managers for a written plan to improve your business**—or at least their own department.

In order to effectively elicit useful information from your people, you need to go about it in a systematic way. Don't simply ask open ended questions. Instead, periodically require each manager to provide written suggestions on what your company can do to:

- help them become better managers;
- make their departments better; and
- make the firm as a whole a better organization.

Don't make it easy for your managers either. Require each of them to come up with at least five solid suggestions in each of those three areas.

The first idea or two that people write down tends to be the obvious ones. The really good, creative suggestions for improving the business come after the individual has spent some time brainstorming.

Invariably, the suggestions you can take to the bank are the fourth or fifth ones that your people will come up with.

There's no telling what ideas will ultimately emerge from this process, but I guarantee you will learn a lot about your own organization. You'll also start your managers thinking in the right direction, and that can pay dividends at any company. Indeed, the basic ideas for every one of the chapters in this book came as a result of exactly this kind of employee brain picking.

It's important, however, that you make sure to let your people know which of their suggestions were adopted, how they were put to use, and why others were rejected. The key is to make them understand that all of their ideas were appreciated and received serious consideration.

STRATEGY NUMBER 81: Brain-Pick Your Key Management Team

HOW DOES THIS APPLY TO MY BUSINESS? _____

_____

_____

_____

_____

Priority   1   2   3   *(circle one)*   Action date _____

Potential dollar effect $ _____

Person assigned to this strategy _____

82. Stamp Out Negative Attitudes Throughout the Organization

A good attitude can work wonders at any organization. A cheerful receptionist, a friendly delivery person, or a sales clerk with a winning smile can be money in the bank for your business.

By the same token, a bad attitude on the part of the employees or managers of a business can drag the organization down like a 500 pound anchor.

Even under the best of conditions your company can't afford to turn off potential clients or chase away customers. When the economy is soft and you're desperately trying to attract business, **there's absolutely no place for anyone with an attitude problem.**

Believe me, negative attitudes can infect an entire organization. I've seen cases where one or two bitter employees have poisoned the thinking of an entire staff.

When business is bad and the company is in trouble, this kind of "Stinkin' Thinkin'" can turn the situation from bad to worse. It's important that top management move quickly to eliminate staff misconceptions and set the record straight. Bring your employees together and level with them.

In one case, the absentee owner of a car dealership was suffering through the worst slump in 20 years. Sales were off sharply, and the overhead was eating the company alive.

The owner made one of his infrequent inspections of the business, and was absolutely shocked to find the place a total mess.

The windows were dirty, the floors were filthy, the cars on the lot hadn't been washed for months, and the employees weren't even bothering to answer the telephones. No wonder sales were off!

When he asked the employees about the condition of the place, he discovered that the source of the problem was the general manager, himself. It seems that this individual had spread lies about the owner to the staff, and fostered discontent throughout the organization.

He even told the employees that our client had refused to pay for a Christmas tree for the showroom—a complete fabrication. For his own reasons, this disgruntled manager almost brought down the company by spreading "Stinkin' Thinkin'" through the staff.

Of course, the owner fired the general manager on the spot, and then called a meeting of the entire staff to spell out the facts of life.

It was the kind of meeting that a lot of troubled businesses should hold every now and then. The owner began by accepting part of the blame himself. He acknowledged that his failure to keep in day to day contact with the business contributed to the "ST."

At the same time, he explained that things were changing, that he expected a high standard of performance from every employee, and that he was confident they could deliver it.

But he also made it clear that if they felt unable or unwilling to perform up to expectations, there were plenty of people who would be happy to fill their shoes.

It was actually a very motivational speech. And the negative staff attitudes evaporated on the spot. During the next ten days, they sold more cars than they had during the previous 30. So much for Stinkin' Thinkin'.

STRATEGY NUMBER 82: Stamp Out Negative Attitudes Throughout the Organization

HOW DOES THIS APPLY TO MY BUSINESS? _____

_____

_____

_____

_____

Priority   1   2   3   *(circle one)*   Action date _____

Potential dollar effect $ _____

Person assigned to this strategy _____

83. Form an Internal Cost-Cutting Committee to Trim Waste

One key to surviving an economic downturn is to eliminate wasteful business practices and other unnecessary expenses. Fortunately, you have a secret weapon in the war against waste: your own employees.

You could bring in a dozen time-and-motion experts with stopwatches and clipboards, but it would take those outsiders weeks to discover what your own people already know!

Even when everything's going right, you should have your ear cocked for suggestions from your staff. When the chips are down and the company is on the ropes, it's doubly important to tap your own employees for solutions.

Of course, you can't just sit back and wait for the answers to pop up out of the company's employee "Suggestion Box." Before your people can come up with solutions, they need to know what the organization's problems are.

A lot of businesses have found that the best way to generate staff suggestions on eliminating waste is to set up an internal cost-cutting committee. The makeup of such a panel is critical. Too often, people assigned to solving company problems are so wrapped up in their own job duties and responsibilities that they fail to recognize the more global concerns of the organization.

To counteract this sort of tunnel vision, it's a good idea to **staff your committee with representatives from various departments and divisions.** By securing broad, multi-disciplined representation on your internal task force, you can encourage fresh viewpoints and creative solutions.

A large construction company can testify to the benefits of getting fresh perspectives from your employees. This particular company engages in a variety of different types of specialized construction work—everything from road work, to commercial construction, to residential building. Different cost estimators are assigned to each specialized department. In addition to preparing bids on jobs, these estimators are responsible for determining the cost of all materials and sub-contract work for each project.

Individually, each of the estimators was doing a good job of getting the best value on materials and labor for his particular division. But nobody was looking at the situation from the standpoint of the company as a whole.

A decision was made to hire a procurement director, who promptly set up a committee composed of the estimators from each of the divisions. At the first meeting, it quickly became apparent that the lack of central coordination had cost the company dearly.

One division was buying materials from several local distributors. Another was dealing directly with key manufacturers. Still another was buying much of its materials from local building supply outlets. By coordinating purchases and buying from a single designated supplier, the company could achieve significant economies of scale.

In addition to obtaining volume discounts, the company was able to negotiate more favorable payment terms and delivery schedules. The firm also reduced construction site waste significantly as a result of the committee's coordination. Instead of disposing of left-over building materials at the end of a job, this surplus is now shuttled to other divisions where building projects are still underway.

These changes alone save the company more than $200,000 a year. And the suggestions for cost savings are still coming in.

STRATEGY NUMBER 83: Form an Internal Cost-Cutting Committee to Trim Waste
HOW DOES THIS APPLY TO MY BUSINESS? _____

_____

_____

_____

_____

Priority   1   2   3   *(circle one)*   Action date _____
Potential dollar effect $ _____
Person assigned to this strategy _____

84. Trim Training Costs with a Procedures Manual

In good times as well as bad, one of the biggest hidden expenses for many businesses is the cost of bringing new workers up to speed or training existing employees for new job duties.

If your company is anything larger than a mom and pop operation, I can almost guarantee that it's costing a lot more than you think to train employees. This won't show up as a line item on any ledger, but that doesn't mean these expenses don't exist. And it certainly doesn't mean that you shouldn't be taking action to control these costs in a bad economy.

A detailed jobs procedures manual is one of the most direct routes to lower employee training costs. Don't confuse an occupational procedures manual with a job description—another valuable tool for any organization. Job descriptions outline the duties to be performed by employees. A procedures manual explains how to do those jobs.

Such a manual can be extremely useful in recruiting and interviewing job applicants. But more importantly, it can streamline employee training and allow new people to become productive more quickly. The out-of-pocket payroll savings alone can be substantial.

Suppose it takes eight weeks to bring a new employee up to speed in a particular job, and the person's supervisor must devote 25 percent of his or her time to training during that break-in period. A good procedures manual should reduce the necessary training time by at least 20 percent.

At, say $10 per hour for the new employee, and $20 an hour for the supervisor, in the example above the training time costs would come to $4,800 ($10 X 40 hours X 8 weeks = $3,200 + $20 X 40 hours X 8 weeks X 25 percent = $1,600). A 20 percent reduction in training costs would save you nearly $1,000 for each new worker—enough in itself to justify the effort involved in developing a procedures manual.

Aside from these training cost-savings, there are other reasons to develop a procedures manual for your organization. Indeed, the very process of preparing such a manual can provide invaluable insight into the operations of your business. You'll be surprised, and maybe even shocked at what you will learn!

Inevitably, you will discover that your people are doing things a particular way for no reason other than that's the way their predecessor did them.

A large non-profit organization developed a procedures manual for its staff. The process was a real eye-opener. In preparing the manual, the managers discovered that the group's accounting department would routinely log each incoming check in a cash-receipt journal, then photocopy it as a safeguard.

This organization depends on outside donations for funds, and it receives an enormous number of checks in the mail. It took one clerk four hours every day just to photocopy the daily influx of checks.

But it was all wasted time! All the information about the contributors had already been recorded in the journal, so copying the checks served no purpose!

Nobody was sure how or when this senseless procedure began, but it had been going on for at least ten years. In effect, the organization wasted the equivalent of one employee's salary for five years—$125,000!

If it were not for the procedures manual, this waste would still be taking place.

STRATEGY NUMBER 84: Trim Training Costs With a Procedures Manual

HOW DOES THIS APPLY TO MY BUSINESS? _____

_____

_____

_____

_____

Priority   1   2   3   *(circle one)*   Action date _____

Potential dollar effect $ _____

Person assigned to this strategy _____

85. Eliminate Unproductive Meetings

When business is soft, most companies are quick to cut back on travel and entertainment costs, tighten up their procurement procedures, and reduce spending for "non-essentials."

But at many firms, the biggest single overhead item is labor. And what many business owners don't realize is that **wasting labor can drain a company's profits just as fast as wasting supplies or inventory.**

Suppose your department managers work like beavers, ten hours a day, six days a week. But at the same time, let's assume that 20 minutes of their day is spent on pointless or non-productive activities. In effect, 1/33rd of their work time is wasted.

But it isn't just time that's wasted. They could have spent those 20 minutes generating new business for your company, or reducing costs, or otherwise improving your organization. So in a very real sense, 1/33rd of the salaries that you pay to these people is wasted.

If you pay these department heads an average of $60,000 annually, those non-productive 20 minutes a day are costing your business almost $2,000 a year per manager.

To be sure, you can't eliminate all wasted time on the job. But you certainly can make sure that the policies and procedures you require your people to follow aren't wasting time!

At many organizations, the leading cause of wasted staff time is poorly planned and administered meetings.

Some businesses seem to have meetings all the time—whether they're needed or not. Every employee is assigned to six different internal committees, and they all meet three times a week for long, rambling sessions at which nothing seems to get resolved.

If a supervisor who wastes 20 minutes a day can cost you almost $2,000 a year, imagine the cost of a pointless, 2 hour daily meeting involving a dozen employees! More to the point, imagine how much more productive and efficient your organization would be if you stopped squandering the equivalent of 24 hours of executive brainpower every day!

Make no mistake—I'm not saying that meetings don't serve a purpose. Internal communication and planning is critical to any business. But make sure your staff meetings are effective. Here's how:

1. *Set an agenda.* Scheduling a meeting without an agenda is like trying to drive cross-country without a road map. You'll get where you're going eventually—but not without a lot of wrong turns, blind alleys and detours. An agenda, on the other hand, keeps you on track.

2. *Table off-track issues.* If an extraneous issue pops up in a meeting,

resist the urge to pursue it. If it's important enough, schedule it for discussion at a future meeting.

3. *Designate a chairman.* Without someone to take charge of the session and keep the discussion on track, the meeting is almost certain to ramble. I'm not saying you need a parliamentarian with a powdered wig every time three or four employees sit down for a discussion. Typically, the meeting participants will defer to the highest ranking "general" in the room. But at a meeting where all the participants are "lieutenant colonels," one should be designated to chair the session.

4. *Set the meeting length in advance.* It's important to let participants know how long a meeting is likely to last so they can schedule their day. If people are given unlimited time to speak on a subject, they just may take it.

5. *Keep notes of the discussion.* It's a good practice to have a secretary sit in on meetings to keep notes on what was discussed and what was decided. Six months or a year after the meeting, it might be important to know how a particular decision was reached, or why one course of action was approved instead of another.

6. *Let participants plan the next meeting.* At many companies, the agenda for the next meeting is set at the conclusion of the current session. This can save time by enabling the participants to provide input while issues are fresh in everyone's mind.

NAME OF GROUP
MEETING DATE AND TIME
AGENDA

1. Past Topics Revisited
  a. Topic/Speaker
  b. Topic/Speaker
  c. Topic/Speaker

2. Current Topics
  a. Topic/Speaker
  b. Topic/Speaker
  c. Topic/Speaker

3. Open Discussion

4. Good & Welfare (recognition of others in the group for extraordinary contributions to a particular project or to the firm in general)

5. Suggestions for the Next Meeting

STRATEGY NUMBER 85: Eliminate Unproductive Meetings
HOW DOES THIS APPLY TO MY BUSINESS? _____
_____
_____
_____
_____

Priority   1   2   3   *(circle one)*   Action date _____
Potential dollar effect $ _____
Person assigned to this strategy _____

86. Evaluate Staff Productivity Objectively

No business can afford to carry people who can't or won't pull their own weight. In addition to the obvious drain on your company's scarce resources, unproductive employees tend to have a demoralizing effect on the rest of your staff. Keeping a slacker on the payroll is a slap in the face for all your hard working employees.

Remember: your organization is only as strong as its weakest link. Your job is to **find the "weak links" by measuring the productivity of your employees.**

Too many managers evaluate staff performance subjectively. Develop an objective yardstick to measure the productivity of your employees and you may be surprised at what you discover. Some people you regarded as only marginal employees may be among your "Most Valuable Players." Conversely, the ones you thought were the company "stars" may not be "MVPs" after all.

There are dozens of different ways to measure employee performance objectively. You can develop statistics showing how much each worker produces, sells, delivers, or collects for your firm. You can analyze staffers based on their attendance record, customer complaint history, overtime wages, travel and entertainment spending, or fifty other variables.

A retailer, struggling through a sluggish business period, was able to turn things around completely by undertaking a more effective analysis of staff productivity.

This particular store employed about 60 salespeople, who earned salaries and commissions averaging $30,000 each. As sales continued to decline, it became increasingly difficult for the retailer to justify this $1.8 million payroll.

Belatedly, the owner undertook an analysis of sales and profitability by employee, and discovered a wide range of performance among his sales staff. Indeed, about one-third of his people were carrying two-thirds of the weight!

At our suggestion, the owner eliminated the dead wood, brought in some talented newcomers, and upgraded his veteran "MVPs." He wound up with a much smaller staff of 30, but they were all highly motivated professionals who were earning an average of $40,000 each—about 30 percent above the "going rate" for the industry.

Even at the higher salaries, however, the store's total payroll costs dropped by a third, thanks to the staff reductions. Best of all, the new "tighter ship" was also a more productive one. Within a year the new, more highly motivated sales staff increased revenues 25 percent, and generated $750,000 in additional gross profit for the business.

Coupled with the $600,000 the company saved in labor costs, plus even more savings from reduced payroll taxes and fringe benefit costs, the company managed to improve its bottom line by more than $1,350,000!

Not bad in a weak economy!

SAMPLE WORK TEAM PERFORMANCE EVALUATION

1. Individual demonstrated a positive and professional approach toward work.

Initials of work team members						
• Always						
• Usually						
• Sometimes						
• Never						

2. The individual responded to your questions in a way that produced results.

Initials of work team members						
• Always						
• Usually						
• Sometimes						
• Never						

3. The individual scheduled time to direct the work and kept you aware of changes in the assignment.

Initials of work team members						
• Always						
• Usually						
• Sometimes						
• Never						

4. The individual acted as a team player in working on the completion of the project.

Initials of work team members						
• Always						
• Usually						
• Sometimes						
• Never						

5. The individual displayed a positive attitude towards the firm.

Initials of work team members						
• Always						
• Usually						
• Sometimes						
• Never						

6. The individual had adequate knowledge of internal and external resources to provide adequate direction for your assignment.

Initials of work team members						
• Excellent						
• Good						
• Fair						
• Unsatisfactory						

7. The individual responded to your questions by assisting you in developing a strategy to solve the problem.

Initials of work team members						
• Excellent						
• Good						
• Fair						
• Unsatisfactory						

8. The individual encouraged you to accept additional responsibility and to work to your potential.

Initials of work team members						
• Excellent						
• Good						
• Fair						
• Unsatisfactory						

9. Whenever possible the individual included you in the planning job.

Initials of work team members						
• Excellent						
• Good						
• Fair						
• Unsatisfactory						

10. The individual was open-minded to your suggestions.

Initials of work team members						
• Excellent						
• Good						
• Fair						
• Unsatisfactory						

11. The individual worked with you so the job was carefully and thoroughly planned by both of you.

Initials of work team members						
• Excellent						
• Good						
• Fair						
• Unsatisfactory						

12. The individual worked with you to develop a reliable and analytical approach to problem solving.

Initials of work team members						
• Excellent						
• Good						
• Fair						
• Unsatisfactory						

13. The individual communicated in an understandable manner.

Initials of work team members						
• Excellent						
• Good						
• Fair						
• Unsatisfactory						

14. The individual was clear in defining the ground rules being used in the decision making, i.e. the level of input you would have in the decision.

Initials of work team members						
• Excellent						
• Good						
• Fair						
• Unsatisfactory						

15. In a group environment (i.e. team meeting, quality control meeting, etc.) did the individual contribute, direct, and help to sustain the objectives of the group?

Initials of work team members						
• Excellent						
• Good						
• Fair						
• Unsatisfactory						

16. When the individual was required to display job expertise he/she was up-to-date, thorough, interested, resourceful and creative.

Initials of work team members						
• Always						
• Usually						
• Sometimes						
• Never						

17. From a technical point of view the individual was independent, and used creative thinking while supervising a job.

Initials of work team members						
• Excellent						
• Good						
• Fair						
• Unsatisfactory						

18. From an economic point of view, did the individual take steps to minimize the expenses to the firm and to the client while maintaining quality and service (i.e. exhibit entrepreneurial skills)?

Initials of work team members					
• Always					
• Usually					
• Sometimes					
• Never					

19. The individual wrote and spoke in a clear and concise manner.

Initials of work team members					
• Excellent					
• Good					
• Fair					
• Unsatisfactory					

20. The individual delegated work to you effectively.

Initials of work team members						
• Excellent						
• Good						
• Fair						
• Unsatisfactory						

21. The individual made you want to excel and succeed with the firm.

Initials of work team members						
• Always						
• Usually						
• Sometimes						
• Never						

22. The individual encouraged you to accept challenges and set high goals.

Initials of work team members						
• Excellent						
• Good						
• Fair						
• Unsatisfactory						

23. The individual provided you with adequate feedback on the job.

Initials of work team members						
• Excellent						
• Good						
• Fair						
• Unsatisfactory						

24. The individual took actions to improve your performance.

Initials of work team members						
• Excellent						
• Good						
• Fair						
• Unsatisfactory						

25. The individual complied with the profession's and the firm's standards.

Initials of work team members						
• Excellent						
• Good						
• Fair						
• Unsatisfactory						

26. Did the individual demonstrate enthusiasm and actions in support of the firm's motto?

Initials of work team members						
• Always						
• Usually						
• Sometimes						
• Never						

27. Did the individual set the example of assisting our clients through difficult economic times as set forth in our mission statement?

Initials of work team members						
• Always						
• Usually						
• Sometimes						
• Never						

28. The individual supported firm decisions.

Initials of work team members						
• Always						
• Usually						
• Sometimes						
• Never						

29. Did the individual provide constructive criticisms which helped you to develop your strengths?

Initials of work team members						
• Always						
• Usually						
• Sometimes						
• Never						

30. When new duties were assigned (i.e. promotion, new job assignments) were the new duties and responsibilities adequately explained?

Initials of work team members						
• Excellent						
• Good						
• Fair						
• Unsatisfactory						

31. Was the individual's year-round discussion of your work consistent with the annual evaluation?

Initials of work team members						
• Excellent						
• Good						
• Fair						
• Unsatisfactory						

32. Was there a feeling that both you and the individual were responsible for your advancements?

Initials of work team members						
• Always						
• Usually						
• Sometimes						
• Never						

33. Did the individual assist you in developing closer relationships with clients?

Initials of work team members						
• Always						
• Usually						
• Sometimes						
• Never						

34. Was the individual able to identify trends and opportunities in practices, marketing efforts, potential areas for new business, etc.

Initials of work team members					
• Excellent					
• Good					
• Fair					
• Unsatisfactory					

35. Did the individual help you to understand marketing and your role in the process?

Initials of work team members					
• Always					
• Usually					
• Sometimes					
• Never					

36. Did the individual help you to understand the firm and its resources?

Initials of work team members						
• Always						
• Usually						
• Sometimes						
• Never						

37. Did the individual help you to improve your personal communication skills, both written and oral?

Initials of work team members						
• Always						
• Usually						
• Sometimes						
• Never						

38. Overall, did the individual display effective management leadership and entrepreneurial skills?

Initials of work team members						
• Always						
• Usually						
• Sometimes						
• Never						

Additional Comments:

_____

_____

_____

_____

_____

_____

_____

_____

_____

_____

_____

_____

_____

_____

_____

_____

_____

_____

STRATEGY NUMBER 86: Evaluate Staff Productivity Objectively

HOW DOES THIS APPLY TO MY BUSINESS? _____

_____

_____

_____

_____

Priority   1   2   3   *(circle one)*   Action date _____

Potential dollar effect $ _____

Person assigned to this strategy _____

87. Seize Opportunities to Upgrade Your Staff

The team that wins the Superbowl is regarded as the best in the league. But even Superbowl winners draft new players and make off-season trades to strengthen their organizations.

Why? Because you don't get ahead by standing still. It's the same in business. You need the best people you can get just to keep pace with the competition. And that goes double during a bad economy.

If there's a silver lining to anything as disruptive as a recession, it's that these economic conditions may enable you to add some real "All-Stars" to your team.

In normal times, recruiting good employees can be a major challenge, and finding great ones might be all but impossible. But **in a depressed economy there may be a surplus of excellent prospects available**—people who can help your company survive the hard times and prosper in the good.

When first-rate people are pounding the pavement looking for employment, there's just no justification to keep poor workers in your organization.

Indeed, a weak economy may offer you a golden opportunity to upgrade your staff and get rid of the slackers, trouble-makers, dishonest employees, people who can't or won't learn to do their job properly.

I was making this point recently in a lecture to business owners when one person in the audience abruptly stood up and walked out of the room.

After the meeting I asked her whether I had said something that disturbed her. "On the contrary," she replied. "Your talk inspired me to make some long overdue staff improvements at my company."

It seems several employees in her organization had not been doing their jobs for almost a year. Despite repeated warnings, these people were just not making a contribution to the firm. The owner had been meaning to discharge these individuals months ago, but kept putting off the unpleasant task.

My point about the availability of first-string job prospects struck a nerve with her, and galvanized her into action. She left the room in the middle of my talk, marched straight to a telephone and called in orders to terminate the unwanted employees.

"What a relief," she told me later. "I feel like I just put down an 80 pound suitcase!"

She felt even better a few weeks later when she saw all the top-notch applicants eager to work at her firm.

STRATEGY NUMBER 87: Seize Opportunities to Upgrade Your Staff

HOW DOES THIS APPLY TO MY BUSINESS? _____

_____

_____

_____

_____

Priority   1   2   3   *(circle one)*   Action date _____

Potential dollar effect $ _____

Person assigned to this strategy _____

88. Cross-train Employees to Handle Multiple Job Duties

Cutting dead wood is easy. But what if your survival requires you to eliminate "indispensable" employees? What happens to your organization if you have to lay off the only person who knows how to operate the switchboard? Or the only one who knows how to use the computer software?

Even in the best of times, it's not wise to have only one person in the office who knows how the filing system is organized, or how to keep the books, or where to go to purchase supplies and inventory.

In a bad economic climate, it's just tempting fate to have only one person who knows how to fix things, or write proposals, or who to call for goods or services. The answer is to keep your options open by **cross-training employees to perform multiple duties.**

Cross-training doesn't have to be a big production. Ask your experienced employees, for instance, to train new personnel in several job skills. Your employees can also write instruction booklets or procedure manuals outlining the nuts and bolts of their jobs.

Although it's an insurance policy in bad times, cross-training will also come in handy when the recession fades and you've got an extra hand to help out with an increased workload.

Most importantly though, cross-training employees in various job skills is a way to make sure that your organization will never be held hostage by employees who regard themselves as "indispensable." Everyone has heard horror stories about employees who feel they are too good to be let go.

For years, one business suffered with a bookkeeper who knew her job but simply drove everyone in the company crazy. Although she was clearly a disruptive influence on the entire organization, the owner was afraid to let her go because she was the only person in the company who knew the bookkeeping system.

Finally, the owner got the word about cross-training. He urged one of his assistants to learn more about the company's financial record keeping, and after a few months the assistant knew enough to permit the company to "encourage" the bookkeeper to consider "early retirement."

The result was a healthier office atmosphere and a significant payroll saving. The old bookkeeper had been making $70,000 a year. Although the owner offered his assistant a $15,000 raise to replace the bookkeeper, the business was still over $20,000 ahead in payroll savings.

STRATEGY NUMBER 88: Cross-Train Employees to Handle Multiple Job Duties

HOW DOES THIS APPLY TO MY BUSINESS? _____

_____

_____

_____

_____

Priority   1   2   3   *(circle one)*   Action date _____

Potential dollar effect $ _____

Person assigned to this strategy _____

89. Use "Show & Tell" to Shave Staff Educational Costs

Educational seminars and courses are important vehicles for keeping your organization on the cutting edge. These meetings can be a cost-effective way to tune your staff into the latest industry tends, advanced management techniques, key shifts in regulatory requirements, or state-of-the-art business equipment.

Under normal conditions, the payoff from a well-conducted educational seminar can easily justify the cost of sending your key people out of town for a few days.

But when sales are down and cash is short, those expenses become more difficult to absorb.

Many employers are exploring ways to tighten up on expenses associated with these courses. One of the most effective of these is to **have your employees share the know-how they gain from educational seminars.**

One firm now sends only one employee to each educational meeting or seminar. When that person returns, he or she shares the fruits of that course with the rest of the organization at the regular weekly staff meeting. The employees call this process "Show and Tell." The boss calls it a bonanza because it gives the company a lot more bang for the buck.

A law firm implemented a variation of this Show and Tell procedure. The partners at this particular firm were strong believers in encouraging their staff to attend job-related courses and meetings. On an annual basis the firm was spending more than $50,000 for such seminars.

When the attorneys began experiencing cash flow problems and took a close look at these staff educational courses, they discovered a lot of duplication and waste.

Employees in one section of the firm would take courses to gain experience with a new computer software program to handle legal research, for example, but people in another section were totally unaware that this knowledge existed in-house. As a result, the firm had two legal research systems and was not getting its money's worth from the computerized system.

Additionally, the lawyers discovered that they had no system to prevent staffers from wasting time at worthless seminars. One employee would attend such a meeting or course, and two weeks later someone else in the firm would go to the same session without knowing it was a waste.

The attorneys responded by implementing new procedures designed to maximize the firm's return on investment in educational seminars. Now when one of the employees takes a course or attends an educational meeting, he must fill out a detailed evaluation form explaining the positive and negative aspects of the seminar.

That information is then transferred to a staff "education log" which must be reviewed by any employee prior to attending a course or meeting. Based on the information in this log, employees often decide against attending a meeting. Rather, they conclude that it would be enough to simply review the course materials and talk with the staffer who attended the previous session.

As a result, the staff eliminated a lot of wasted time and the firm's annual expenditures for these courses dropped 20 percent from $50,000 to $40,000.

PARTICIPANT'S COURSE EVALUATION

Program Title: _____

Sponsor: _____

Date(s) of Program: _____

Location: _____

Instructor(s): _____

Please indicate your agreement or disagreement with each statement.

	Agree	*Neutral*	*Disagree*
1. The program objectives were met.	☐	☐	☐
2. The program was well-suited to my background, education & experience.	☐	☐	☐
3. The materials were well organized and relevant.	☐	☐	☐
4. The advance preparation was useful in meeting program objectives.	☐	☐	☐
5. The instructor was effective.	☐	☐	☐
6. The meeting room was suitable for the program.	☐	☐	☐
7. Overall, the program was of value to me.	☐	☐	☐
8. I would recommend this course to others in the firm	☐	☐	☐

Please provide a brief description of the course contents that you found to be of value and specific items that you feel would be useful to share with other staff members.

_____

_____

_____

_____

_____

_____

_____

_____

_____

_____

_____

_____

_____

_____

_____

STRATEGY NUMBER 89: Use "Show & Tell" to Shave Staff Educational Costs

HOW DOES THIS APPLY TO MY BUSINESS? _____

_____

_____

_____

_____

Priority   1   2   3   *(circle one)*   Action date _____

Potential dollar effect $ _____

Person assigned to this strategy _____

Part V

Marketing Resources

90. Identify Your Company's Edge in the Marketplace

When an organization is struggling to survive a business downturn, it's easy to forget that every company has strengths as well as weaknesses. Recognizing those strengths and capitalizing on them is every bit as important as eliminating the weaknesses.

Indeed, the mere process of identifying what makes your company a little better than the competition can be a real morale-builder during troubled times.

Make no mistake, every company is special in one way or another. There's something that sets your business apart from the pack.

Your restaurant, for example, may not have a five star rating, but it just might serve the best pot roast in the area.

Similarly, the corner pharmacist may not be able to match the discount prices of the chain store down the street, but by offering to deliver prescriptions night and day, he can carve a niche in the market.

Your company's competitive edge might be something as complex as a state-of-the-art computer system or as simple as having a warm, friendly receptionist.

In a soft economy it's even more important to identify your company's strengths and capitalize on them. Failing to communicate the attributes that make your business special is like entering a boxing ring with one hand tied behind your back. You might come out a winner, but the odds are against it.

Take the case of the office equipment supply house that appeared to be doing everything right. This particular firm offers 24-hour service on all business machines that it sells or leases. Customers receive a free "loaner" whenever their equipment is being repaired. In addition, the company allows businesses to renew maintenance agreements for as long as they own their equipment.

These are really valuable customer services and no other supplier in the area can match them. Yet the company was struggling because of competition from firms that offered less.

The problem was that this business simply was not communicating its strengths to potential clients.

Old customers took these liberal service policies for granted; new ones were never even told of the company's practices; and some of the firm's own employees were unaware that these policies were special.

Fortunately, the owner of this business recognized the problem and took steps to communicate the company's strengths. Today, all prospective customers are supplied with a detailed brochure outlining the company's services and explaining the advantages of dealing with this firm.

The company is still battling for market share, but at least now it's using both fists!

STRATEGY NUMBER 90: Identify Your Company's Edge in the Marketplace

HOW DOES THIS APPLY TO MY BUSINESS? _____

_____

_____

_____

_____

Priority   1   2   3   *(circle one)*   Action date _____

Potential dollar effect $ _____

Person assigned to this strategy _____

91. Maintain Quality Customer Relations

In good times, success can spoil even the most well managed organizations.

When a business is flooded with orders and can pick and choose the jobs it wants, your staff simply may not have as much time to interact with customers as they used to. In some cases, a business "culture" develops in which some employees actually believe "the customer needs our business" instead of "our business needs the customer."

A good recession will bring any company down to earth with a thump. When many competitors are vying for the same business, customers become choosy. After all, why give hard earned cash to any business where the people are less than courteous and attentive?

In a bad economy, **good relations with your customers may be the deciding factor in every sale you make.**

It's been said that you need to do something well at least ten times before a customer will recommend you to a friend. However it only takes one bad experience with a rude salesperson, or a lackadaisical receptionist, or a delivery person with an attitude problem, and that customer will complain about you to ten others.

Eliminating such negative practices is only half the battle, however. To really solidify good relations with your customers you have to deliver more than they expect to receive from you.

Look at it in terms of the following equation:

$$\text{Customer Relations Index} = \frac{\text{Your Company's Product or Service}}{\text{Your Customers' Expectations}}$$

If your company's Customer Relations Index (CRI) is less than 1, you're in trouble. Your customers or clients believe they are being shortchanged.

If your CRI is 1, customer relations at your business are neutral. Your clients are getting what they bargained for—no more, no less.

If the index is more than 1, your business is a winner and so are your customers! It means you're delivering even more than your customers expect.

The wonderful part is that it doesn't have to cost an arm and a leg to move your Customer Relations Index well into the triple digit range.

A luxury car dealer in our community makes it a practice to surprise purchasers of new vehicles with a little extra gift. Along with every new car delivered by this dealer, the customer receives a BMW key ring and a matching baseball cap.

These little keepsakes probably didn't cost the dealer more than $5 or $6, but that's not the point.

The point is that the car buyer was expecting to receive a $30,000 automobile. Instead, the dealer delivered a $30,000 automobile, a key chain and a baseball cap. The result: positive customer relations at the onset of the relationship.

STRATEGY NUMBER 91: Maintain Quality Customer Relations

HOW DOES THIS APPLY TO MY BUSINESS? _____

_____

_____

_____

_____

Priority   1   2   3   *(circle one)*   Action date _____

Potential dollar effect $ _____

Person assigned to this strategy _____

92. Keep Tabs on Your Competitors' Prices

Even in the best of times, it's important to keep close tabs on what your competitors are charging. When business is bad, ensuring that your goods or services are competitively priced is a matter of survival.

Often this entails merely keeping your eyes peeled for newspaper ads placed by your rivals. In other cases, you may have to do a little creative snooping.

A chain of hair salons in a very competitive market, regularly sends key employees out to have their hair done at competing shops. Although no company likes to send business to its rivals, in this case the practice has paid big dividends. The owner's "undercover" customers not only bring back current information on prices being charged by competitors, but also invaluable first-hand feedback on the quality of services being provided by other salons.

Some businesses run into trouble because they price their goods and services too high for the market. During a slumping economy, however, it's more common for problems to arise because prices are set too low.

Don't think you have to be the cheapest guy in town in order to attract business. If your prices or bids are the lowest around, find out whether you're getting business because you're the cheapest, or because you're better than your competitors. If the goods or services offered by your company are high quality, you may well be able to revise your pricing strategy, even in a bad economy.

While you don't want to be significantly more expensive than your competitors, you don't want to be low man on the totem pole, either.

A restaurateur with a reputation for offering great food and excellent service learned this lesson first hand. The place was drawing more business than ever, yet the owner was having only a mediocre year.

He compared other food service establishments in the area and found that he had the lowest menu prices in town. His place was always packed because he served good food—not because he charged low prices. Realizing this, he raised his menu prices by an average of 10 percent without losing any business.

The establishment grosses about $12 million a year, so the price increases brought in an additional $1.2 million. Best of all, since the restaurant incurred no additional costs in order to realize this gain, that entire $1.2 million went straight to the bottom line!

Instead of struggling through another marginal year, the restaurateur's net income more than doubled overnight!

In another case, the owner of a commercial repair business developed a sizeable customer base over the years as a result of word-of-mouth referrals. The owner assumed that his success was due to his practice of underbidding his competitors. When he surveyed his customers, however, he learned that they patronized his business because he provided reliable work, stood behind his repairs, and met deadlines.

The owner raised his prices at least 15 percent and was still competitive with other services in the area. He didn't lose a single customer because of the price hike.

STRATEGY NUMBER 92: Keep Tabs on Your Competitors' Prices

HOW DOES THIS APPLY TO MY BUSINESS? _____

_____

_____

_____

_____

Priority   1   2   3   *(circle one)*   Action date _____

Potential dollar effect $ _____

Person assigned to this strategy _____

93. Monitor Your Competition to Keep on Top of the Market

One of the best sources of information on how to cope with a bad economy may be right under your nose. **If you're suffering and your competitor isn't, maybe the other guy is doing something right!**

But even if your business rivals are in worse shape than you, it's important to check them out. At a minimum, you may be able to learn from their mistakes.

To be sure, it's always wise to keep one eye on the competition. But when business is down, your margin of error becomes slimmer and you can't afford to pass up any potential edge.

An automobile dealer makes it a point to keep close tabs on the activities of the other dealerships in the area. He even gets regular Dun & Bradstreet financial reports on his leading competitors.

Unexpectedly, one of his key rivals slashed prices and began aggressively promoting discounts. Ordinarily, he would have been reluctant to get into a price war—particularly during a soft economy. But because he had the D&B report, the dealer knew that his rival was even less capable to sustain losses for any period of time.

Recognizing the competitor's price cuts as a desperation move, he matched them. Because he had deeper pockets, the dealership not only survived but ultimately broadened his market share.

Securing financial reports on your competitors is only one way to keep on top in the marketplace. Trade publications, industry associations, area business groups such as the local Chamber of Commerce are all excellent sources of information on what's happening in the market.

In addition, you can often get a wealth of information about what your competitors are up to by talking with your suppliers. Hiring employees from the competition may also yield invaluable intelligence.

There's also the direct approach. Just ask other people in your industry what they're doing to stay above water. You would be surprised how helpful other business people can be. Even direct competitors often swap advice when the wolf is at the door.

STRATEGY NUMBER 93: Monitor Your Competition to Keep On Top of the Market

HOW DOES THIS APPLY TO MY BUSINESS? _____

_____

_____

_____

_____

Priority   1   2   3   *(circle one)*   Action date _____

Potential dollar effect $ _____

Person assigned to this strategy _____

94. Adjust Prices to Maximize Profits, Not Sales

When profits plunge, one very direct path back to economic health is to raise your prices. Admittedly, in some industries the competition is so intense that it is very difficult for businesses to raise prices. If every store on the block sells milk at $1 a quart, and you raise your price to $1.10, you could lose half of your customers!

Most businesses, however, are not in industries or markets which are that price sensitive. Yet many business people are fearful of raising prices, even when their company's survival is at stake.

The trick is to **determine the effect of price increases on your business and adjust prices to maximize profits.**

A small jewelry business that specializes in repairs generated about $100,000 annually, but experienced very little earnings growth over the years. It didn't take a genius to figure out why—their price list hadn't been adjusted for nearly a decade! When we questioned the owners about their charges, they said they had to keep their prices "in line" to retain their customers.

The jewelers felt that if they were to follow our advice and raise prices, say 50 percent, they would lose as many as one-third of their customers. "Only a third?" we replied. "That proves our point!"

Indeed, it does. If your current sales are $100,000 and you raise prices 50 percent, you're up to $150,000. Then if you lose one-third of those sales, you're back to $100,000 again.

But, of course, you're not really back where you started. Your cost of goods and other operating expenses has dropped significantly, reflecting the one-third drop in unit sales. The end result is a sizeable increase on the bottom line.

With a great deal of trepidation, the jewelers accepted our reasoning and raised prices just in time for the Christmas season. As it turned out, their business didn't drop by one-third. In fact, they didn't lose any business at all as a result of the price adjustment.

This happy ending is due to the fact that they offer high quality work, fast 24-hour turn-around, and excellent service. The customer who comes in with a $2,000 ring is not likely to argue if the shop charges $30 to size it instead of $20.

In some cases, of course, the way to maximize profits is to lower prices (or at least appear to lower them).

An air conditioning service, for example, slashed its rates by 10 percent and at the same time instituted a new supply charge that averaged out to $4.50 per hour. The company's normal hourly rate was cut from $50 to

$45, and customers really perked up at that reduction. In contrast, they hardly noticed the new supply charge, which effectively brought the rate back up to $49.50.

In reality, the firm had reduced its charges only 1 percent, yet the change triggered a 20 percent increase in sales and a net gain on the bottom line of $100,000.

STRATEGY NUMBER 94: Adjust Prices to Maximize Profits, Not Sales

HOW DOES THIS APPLY TO MY BUSINESS? _____

_____

_____

_____

_____

Priority   1   2   3   *(circle one)*   Action date _____

Potential dollar effect $ _____

Person assigned to this strategy _____

95. Broaden Your Market by "Bundling" Products or Services

I went to the shoe store the other day to buy a pair of oxfords. When I picked them out, the sales clerk suggested that I pick up an extra pair of laces, and some polish. He even called my attention to a sale on argyle socks! Thanks to good old fashioned "suggestive selling," I left the store loaded down with impulse purchases.

In many businesses, however, it's just not possible to have a crack salesman on hand suggesting tie-in purchases. But that doesn't mean you can't generate extra sales volume by 'bundling' related goods or services. **Instead of just one hit, you could get a double or triple sale—maybe even a home run!**

There's a car wash near our office where they offer barebones service for $6. But for $8.95, they will not only wash your car, but vacuum the interior and apply spray wax. Although the big sign out front promotes the $6 wash, most customers choose the package. It's a better value for them, and a more profitable sale for the car wash owner.

Many businesses could broaden their market penetration by trying variations on this same theme. A restaurant, for example, could generate customer interest in particularly profitable menu selections by bundling an appetizer, entree and dessert at a single attractive price.

Similarly, if you operate a service station you could offer an oil change, lube and tire rotation all at a single reduced price. Overall, of course, your profit margin will be lower due to the discount. But in terms of profit *dollars,* you'll be money ahead because many customers will be purchasing additional products and services because of the tie-in.

One entrepreneur developed a terrific recipe for clam chowder. He had the soup canned and began marketing it locally. The response was all right, but sales didn't really take off until he hit on the idea of selling his chowder in six-packs like beer.

Then he realized that almost everybody who bought his clam chowder was a prime customer for oyster crackers. He began packaging crackers with each six-pack, and the result was a nice big bottom line bonus for our client.

STRATEGY NUMBER 95: Broaden Your Market by "Bundling" Products or Services

HOW DOES THIS APPLY TO MY BUSINESS? _____

_____

_____

_____

_____

Priority   1   2   3   *(circle one)*   Action date _____

Potential dollar effect $ _____

Person assigned to this strategy _____

96. Put Yourself in Charge of Customer Relations

When your bottom line is at stake, customer relations aren't just the job of the sales department. They're everyone's responsibility—especially the boss's. When the going gets tough, **business owners should call on customers personally.**

Clients have reason to feel special when the owner or other top management people take the time to visit them personally. I've seen owners rekindle business relationships with customers who were thought to be lost forever.

A lot of this is psychological—the charisma when the owner of one business meets with the owner of another. But there's more to it than that. In many cases, the owner is the company's best salesman. Typically, the boss started out in sales, and he was probably pretty good at it. If the company's founder wasn't a good salesperson to begin with, it's doubtful that the business would have gotten off the ground.

The owner of a glass installation company is just such a salesman. He built the business from scratch, and in the beginning he handled all of the sales.

As the business expanded, he hired a sales staff and devoted his time to management and administration. Things were going fine until the construction market collapsed and with it glass installation sales.

The owner seized the initiative and began accompanying his salespeople on calls. Within three months a number of new customers had signed on and business was up 20 percent.

The owner of a business brings something extra into a sales transaction. A salesman is restricted by company policy, but the boss can bend the rules when necessary to make a sale or solidify relations with a customer.

As the owner of the business, you can offer price concessions, make delivery commitments, authorize returns, and change payment terms on the spot.

STRATEGY NUMBER 96: Put Yourself in Charge of Customer Relations

HOW DOES THIS APPLY TO MY BUSINESS? _____

_____

_____

_____

_____

Priority   1   2   3   *(circle one)*   Action date _____

Potential dollar effect $ _____

Person assigned to this strategy _____

97. Expand Business Hours to Rope In New Customers

When sales are soft and everybody in the market is scratching for customers, arbitrarily turning away business can be the economic equivalent of suicide.

But lots of companies are doing just that. Instead of knuckling down and going after customers, it's business as usual at these places.

You know the people I'm talking about. The plumber who complains about the recession but refuses to work weekends. The physician who can't pay the rent but still plays golf every Tuesday and Friday. The shopkeeper who cries about sluggish sales but still closes the store every day at 5:30.

In a weak economy it's a buyer's market. You can't expect your customers to take valuable time off from their jobs or businesses in order to accommodate your schedule. Sometimes the difference between business success and Chapter 11 is a willingness to **adjust your hours of operation to meet customer demand.**

Look at it this way. If a customer takes time away from a job or business to accommodate your company's schedule, they have to pay double for your services. In addition to what you charge, they may have lost income, to boot.

Why shouldn't you open your office at seven in the morning instead of nine? And why shouldn't you close at seven in the evening instead of 5:30? Would staying open on Saturdays attract more clients?

Customers are often willing to pay a premium for more convenient scheduling. If you could find a plumber or electrician who would commit to doing a job for you at a pre-arranged time, wouldn't that be worth extra? If they could avoid the need to take a day off work to wait for the plumber, I'll bet a lot of people would pay 50 percent extra for that convenience.

The critical question is would expanded hours of operation make it easier for customers to spend their money with your company? For many businesses, the answer is yes.

A service station generated significantly more automobile maintenance business because the owners extended their hours of operation. Under the new schedule, the station began taking cars at 7 a.m. and stayed open until 11 p.m. In fact, customers who dropped their cars off immediately after work were often delighted to have them ready the same evening. That's a real benefit for those who would otherwise have to miss work the next day or find someone to drive them in.

Besides increasing sales at the station by more than 40 percent, this policy created a lot of good will throughout the neighborhood.

Sometimes staying open longer may even open up entire new business opportunities for a company.

A dental practice recently began promoting cosmetic dentistry, such as tooth brightening, as a sideline. The dentist expected this to generate a lot of new and very lucrative business. But the initial reaction from patients was ho-hum. Many people regard cosmetic dentistry as a non-essential procedure—even a vanity. They would take time off from work for a root canal but not for a cosmetic treatment. Fortunately, the dentist recognized this early in the game and hired a young dentist fresh out of school to provide cosmetic dental services in the evenings and on weekends.

The cosmetic practice flourished, and because it was all done during "off-hours," it didn't interfere with the dentist's regular practice. Gravy!

STRATEGY NUMBER 97: Expand Business Hours to Rope In New Customers

HOW DOES THIS APPLY TO MY BUSINESS? _____

_____

_____

_____

_____

Priority   1   2   3   *(circle one)*   Action date _____

Potential dollar effect $ _____

Person assigned to this strategy _____

98. Tap Into Industry Trade Associations

No organization struggling through a rough economic period needs to face adversity alone. If your company is hurting, others in your industry are almost certainly feeling pain as well.

Like your firm, these other businesses are exploring ways to cope with the downturn and prepare for the recovery. The experiences of these companies represent invaluable intelligence on surviving a bad economy and prospering in a good one.

Today there is a trade association, professional society or industry organization to represent virtually every type of business, and these groups offer a wealth of benefits for their members.

The next time you're in the Washington, D.C. area, open the phone book and look under "National Association of . . ." or "American Association of . . ." You will be astonished at the diversity of the industries represented by these groups.

In addition to these national organizations, there are corresponding state and local groups representing a wide range of businesses. These run the gamut from broadly-based chambers of commerce to tightly-focused, industry-specific groups.

Chances are your firm already belongs to one or more of these organizations. But if that's not the case, start checking out the benefits of membership immediately. Almost invariably, our clients have found that **trade associations can be a business lifeline in a sagging economy.**

Many of these organizations prepare detailed operating statistics for business in their industry, and these can serve as invaluable yardsticks for companies struggling in a bad economy.

Comparing your sales per employee, or gross profit per advertising dollar with the average of other firms in your industry can help you identify the strengths and weaknesses of your business. That alone can justify the cost of membership in these organizations.

Additionally, however, trade associations provide a variety of other benefits to members. Typically, these groups offer:

• Educational meetings or seminars to sharpen the skills of your employees;

• Industry newsletters and publications containing valuable business information;

• A structure for influencing regulatory or legislative activity affecting your company; and

• Pre-packaged employee insurance programs and other group "fringe benefits."

Most importantly, though, industry associations offer the opportunity to share experiences, problems and solutions with other businesses in your field.

In a weak economy, you have plenty to do just to keep your company on track. Don't waste time trying to re-invent the wheel.

STRATEGY NUMBER 98: Tap Into Industry Trade Associations

HOW DOES THIS APPLY TO MY BUSINESS? _____

_____

_____

_____

_____

Priority   1   2   3   *(circle one)*   Action date _____

Potential dollar effect $ _____

Person assigned to this strategy _____

99. Cash in on Hard Economic Times

In the first 98 chapters of this book we have focused largely on survival strategies for organizations struggling to stay afloat in a bad economy. But not all businesses are in that boat. Some companies seem to thrive during a general economic downturn .

At our firm we don't just seek to heal sick businesses. We also strive to help our healthy clients become even stronger. Indeed, we have a plaque on our wall that spells out our commitment in the form of a "Mission Statement." It reads as follows:

"A Good Recession Only Comes Along Several Times in a Business Cycle. It is our Responsibility to Assist our Clients in Achieving and Maintaining Profitability."

By this we mean that **during a recession there are tremendous opportunities available to those businesses savvy enough to recognize and act on them.** This book is literally peppered with examples of business men and women who faced down adversity and turned a difficult situation into an advantage for their organizations.

As a result, these businesses are stronger now than they were before the recession, and they are poised to become stronger still during the prosperous years ahead.

The way I look at it, during a downturn businesses tend to fall into one of three categories:

1. Organizations that must focus all of their energies on survival;
2. Those that see the opportunities that arise during a business slow-down and accelerate into new markets or product lines;
3. Those that pounce on their struggling competitors and buy them out, move in on their territories or attract their best employees.

The difference between these three often boils down to the mind-set of the business owner. Some people become overly cautious during an economic downturn. Even if their business is doing all right, they are reluctant to explore new opportunities or take calculated risks.

Others, however, find ways to turn a business downturn into an advantage for their companies. When economic conditions force interest rates down, they cash in by refinancing debt. When the commercial real estate market tumbles, they relocate facilities to secure lower rents. And when sales of existing lines stagnate, they add new products or services to capitalize on the changing realities of the marketplace.

Our firm represents the owner of an automobile dealership—an industry that suffers more than most during any economic slump. While other dealers in his area were moaning and groaning, our client was drawing up plans to accelerate his company out of the recession.

Although the economic climate had made it difficult to sell new cars, the owner recognized that there was a large and growing demand for inexpensive used cars. Indeed, the worse the economy became, the more he encountered financially-strapped people in need of cheap wheels.

He responded by setting up a subsidiary that offered to finance older, high-mileage cars to people with bad credit. These were vehicles that the dealer would otherwise have had to wholesale out at next to nothing. Instead, he had customers banging down his doors to pay top dollar for these automobiles!

At the same time, he was providing a real service to the community! People were able to find cars they could afford, and build up their credit standing. A few years down the road, those same people may be in the market for a new car, and our client will have the inside track!

When economic conditions cut into the demand for your products or services, develop new products or services more in tune with the new marketplace realities.

My brother, Ron, is one of the best real estate attorneys in our state. But when the bottom fell out of the real estate market and his practice dried up, he developed expertise in a new legal specialty tailor-made to the times: bankruptcy law.

STRATEGY NUMBER 99: Cash In on Hard Economic Times

HOW DOES THIS APPLY TO MY BUSINESS? _____

_____

_____

_____

_____

Priority   1   2   3   *(circle one)*   Action date _____

Potential dollar effect $ _____

Person assigned to this strategy _____

100. Stretch Your Advertising Dollars

There's an old saw in retailing that says you don't have to rent a hall to give away merchandise.

That's true in other businesses, too. With a little ingenuity and some elbow grease, you may be able to spread the word about your business without a megaton advertising campaign.

The key is creativity. You should start thinking beyond conventional advertising methods—newspapers, magazines, radio and television. These media are terrific vehicles for promoting a business, and no doubt they're very cost-effective in a healthy economy.

But when your business is suffering from chronic cash shortages, it's difficult to justify such costs. Sometimes, the smartest thing to do is simply holster your guns and save your promotional ammunition for a more effective time.

One furniture store cut its promotional budget to the bone when the economy hit rock bottom. The owner recognized that luxury furniture just doesn't move in a bad economy. This merchant could have tripled his advertising budget, without selling one more recliner or sofa.

On the other hand, for other businesses, promotional efforts may be even more important during a downturn. Advertising just might be the growth stimulant you need to ensure a bumper crop. But if you can't afford to buy the seed, it's hard to justify money for fertilizer.

If that's the situation at your company, it's time to **explore alternatives to stretch your advertising dollars.**

Our firm, for instance, recently signed up for a state-sponsored "Adopt-A-Road" program. The gist of the program is that to "adopt" a road—in our case the main thoroughfare in front of our firm—a business is responsible for keeping the roadsides clean. Our staff goes out about four times a year to pick up trash, and afterwards we reward them with a "post-garbage" party!

What we get in return are several large road signs, courtesy of the state highway service, which acknowledge that the road has been adopted by our firm.

The signs face in both directions of the road, in plain view of the more than 140,000 vehicles that pass by every day. That's free advertising you can take to the bank! In addition to the exposure, our firm is generating a lot of good will in our community for keeping the highway clean.

Another public service activity that we are involved in is to assign accountants to provide free tax information over a telephone hot line. We do this every tax season in cooperation with a local radio station. One day a week, WTOP radio announces every 20 minutes that CPAs from our firm will be manning the phone lines to answer questions from the public about tax filings. It's a real service to many people in our area, and it's wonderful free publicity for our firm.

There are hundreds of things that your organization could do right now to help your community and generate publicity at the same time.

Why not have a blood drive in your office? All you do is volunteer the space, and the Red Cross does the rest. It won't take up office time, because it can be done in the evening, or on the weekend. Most importantly, the media attention you get will save you a couple of thousand in advertising. After all, newspapers, television and radio stations frequently announce local blood drives—including the location and business that is the sponsor. Best of all, your company blood might well end up saving a life!

Another inexpensive alternative to conventional advertising is to develop a newsletter or other communications vehicle to reach potential clients.

A physical therapy clinic launched such a newsletter, which is sent to local medical practitioners. Physicians play a tremendous role in directing patients to physical therapists, and because this particular clinic made its presence known, more doctors are sending them their patients.

When you consider a simple desktop newsletter costs as little as 50 cents per person, you can see the benefits outweigh the expense.

I must add that this newsletter has also yielded some promotional value for our firm. We write a column in the letter on tax tips for medical doctors, and in return we get our name and address published with the article. This kind of freelance writing may not pay anything, but we might walk away with a few doctors who need their taxes done!

STRATEGY NUMBER 100: Stretch Your Advertising Dollars
HOW DOES THIS APPLY TO MY BUSINESS? _____

_____

_____

_____

_____

Priority   1   2   3   *(circle one)*   Action date _____
Potential dollar effect $ _____
Person assigned to this strategy _____

101. POSTSCRIPT — Who's Who in the "100 Ways"

No book entitled *100 Ways to Prosper in Today's Economy* would be complete without a final chapter acknowledging the source of this information and the people behind it.

Indeed, the surest way **not to prosper in any kind of economy is to fail to recognize the people who make your accomplishments possible.**

This book, and the ideas in it, are the fruits of the collective experience and expertise of the accountants and administrative staffers of our firm.

There are also some "aliens" without whose energy and expertise *100 Ways to Prosper in Today's Economy* would be only a list instead of a book.

Veteran business writer Ken Rankin and his associate Wendy Driscoll were the wordsmiths who crafted our thoughts into digestible prose.

Lee Barrett and the members of TEC 122 served as both a sounding board for the ideas in this book, as well as a source for many of them. Indeed, they challenged me to write this book.

The people at Acropolis Books—and publisher Kathleen Hughes in particular—deserve recognition for their support and encouragement of this project from the onset.

Thanks to the most patient family I know: my own. My dear mother, Jane Schimel, and my late father, Leo Schimel, CPA, supported and encouraged me over the years in many more than 100 ways.

I owe a double acknowledgment to my supportive wife Elinor, my daughter and horseback riding buddy, Louise, and my son and friend, Danny. In addition to their emotional support, they all contributed ideas that improved the content of this book.

I want to give special recognition for the support and encouragement of Keith Fetridge, CPA, and other members of Aronson, Fetridge, Weigle & Schimel, who have assisted me in taking the "100 Ways" to new plateaus. If the ideas in this book help you and your business to prosper, these are the people from our firm whom you should thank: Mel Lieberman, CPA, shareholder; Bob Bender, CPA, shareholder; Alex Brager, CPA, shareholder; Jay Abrahams, CPA; Alex Borowsky, CPA; Mark Boyd, CPA; Virginia Breeden; Kimberly Burns; Terry Caherty, CPA; Denise Christenson; Robert Driver, CPA; William Eisig, CPA; Karen Gaskin, CPA; Richard Goldstein, CPA; Donna Hopkins, CPA; Carolyn Knipe, CPA; Christine Lederer; Bruce Lewis, CPA; Suzanne Litchfield; Carol Milwit; Jeanie Motsinger; Lois Rankin; Gary Saber; Keith Thompson; Cynthia Williams, CPA; Mary Zimbelman, CPA.

"100 Ways to Prosper" Master Action Plan for _____

(Name of Company)

List each of the strategies that applies to your business and complete the columns as indicated. When you've finished, you'll have a Master Action Plan ready to put to work for your business.

Strategy Number	Priority 1-2-3	Potential Dollar Effect	Person assigned to Manage this task	Action Date	Additional Comments
1					
2					
3					
4					
5					
6					
7					
8					
9					
10					
11					
12					
13					
14					
15					
16					

Strategy Number	Priority 1-2-3	Potential Dollar Effect	Person assigned to Manage this task	Action Date	Additional Comments
17					
18					
19					
20					
21					
22					
23					
24					
25					
26					
27					
28					
29					
30					
31					
32					
33					
34					
35					
36					
37					
38					
39					
40					
41					
42					

Strategy Number	Priority 1-2-3	Potential Dollar Effect	Person assigned to Manage this task	Action Date	Additional Comments
43					
44					
45					
46					
47					
48					
49					
50					
51					
52					
53					
54					
55					
56					
57					
58					
59					
60					
61					
62					
63					
64					
65					
66					
67					
68					

Strategy Number	Priority 1-2-3	Potential Dollar Effect	Person assigned to Manage this task	Action Date	Additional Comments
69					
70					
71					
72					
73					
74					
75					
76					
77					
78					
79					
80					
81					
82					
83					
84					
85					
86					
87					
88					
89					
90					
91					
92					
93					
94					

Strategy Number	Priority 1-2-3	Potential Dollar Effect	Person assigned to Manage this task	Action Date	Additional Comments
95					
96					
97					
98					
99					
100					

Index

100 WAYS TO PROSPER
IN TODAY'S ECONOMY™
Additional Opportunities for Success

Thank you for purchasing **100 Ways to Prosper in Today's Economy**™. We hope you enjoy the book and take advantage of the other opportunities the "100 Ways"™ offers.

The "100 Ways"™ Workshop

The "100 Ways"™ workshop coaches your organization's decision makers in developing business strategies that we guarantee will enhance profitability.

- Two-day interactive, hands-on workshop tailored to your organization's needs
- Battle-tested strategies to help you prosper through the recession and beyond
- Re-energize, revitalize, and re-invigorate the key decision makers
- Develop an action plan to track and monitor strategies developed during the workshop

The "100 Ways"™ workshops have added tens of millions of dollars to the bottom line of hundreds of organizations.

Other "100 Ways"™ Opportunities

We speak at conventions, conferences, trades shows, and facilitate discussion groups. We tailor the programs to the needs of the business, trade association or not-for-profit organization, presenting a spectrum of ideas that guarantee a financially beneficial program.

Please check the "100 Ways"™ opportunities that are most advantageous to your organization and return this form to: **Aronson, Fetridge, Weigle and Schimel, 6116 Executive Blvd., Fifth Floor, Rockville, Maryland 20852, Attn: Lois Rankin (301/231-6200)** along with the following information:

I would like additional information on the "100 Ways"™ . . .
❑ *workshop* ❑ *speakers.*

NAME: _____

TITLE: _____

COMPANY: _____

TYPE OF COMPANY: _____

ADDRESS: _____

_____

PHONE: _____

Thank you. We will be contacting you with the information you have requested.